797,885 Books
are available to read at

www.ForgottenBooks.com

Forgotten Books' App
Available for mobile, tablet & eReader

ISBN 978-1-330-03875-8
PIBN 10010372

This book is a reproduction of an important historical work. Forgotten Books uses state-of-the-art technology to digitally reconstruct the work, preserving the original format whilst repairing imperfections present in the aged copy. In rare cases, an imperfection in the original, such as a blemish or missing page, may be replicated in our edition. We do, however, repair the vast majority of imperfections successfully; any imperfections that remain are intentionally left to preserve the state of such historical works.

Forgotten Books is a registered trademark of FB &c Ltd.
Copyright © 2015 FB &c Ltd.
FB &c Ltd, Dalton House, 60 Windsor Avenue, London, SW19 2RR.
Company number 08720141. Registered in England and Wales.

For support please visit www.forgottenbooks.com

1 MONTH OF FREE READING

at

www.ForgottenBooks.com

By purchasing this book you are eligible for one month membership to ForgottenBooks.com, giving you unlimited access to our entire collection of over 700,000 titles via our web site and mobile apps.

To claim your free month visit:

www.forgottenbooks.com/free10372

* Offer is valid for 45 days from date of purchase. Terms and conditions apply.

Similar Books Are Available from
www.forgottenbooks.com

The Call of the Surf
by Van Campen Heilner

A Book on Angling
Being a Complete Treatise on the Art of Angling in Every Branch, by Francis Francis

Kinks
A Book of 250 Helpful Hints for Hunters, Anglers and Outers, by Harry N. Katz

Practical Fly Fishing
by Larry St. John

The Determined Angler and the Brook Trout
An Anthological Volume of Trout, by Charles Bradford

The Complete Angler
by Izaak Walton

Routledge's Handbook of Fishing
With Illustrations, by George Routledge

Rambles With a Fishing-Rod
by Edward Stanley Roscoe

Salmon Fishing
by W. Earl Hodgson

Favorite Fish and Fishing
by James A. Henshall

A Book of Fishing Stories
by Frederick G. Aflalo

An Angler's Year
by Charles S. Patterson

Science of Fishing
by Lake Brooks

Anecdotes of Fish and Fishing
by Thomas Boosey

Coarse Fishing
by H. T. Sheringham

What I Have Seen While Fishing and How I Have Caught My Fish
by Philip Geen

Fishing at Home & Abroad
by Herbert Maxwell

Fishing With a Worm
by Bliss Perry

Trout-Fishing for the Beginner
by Richard Clapham

North-Country Flies
Comprising Eleven Plates of Hand-Painted Illustrations, by Thomas Evan Pritt

SH
605
S47
1883
FISH

ISSUED BY AUTHORITY

HANDBOOKS
Issued in connection with
The Great International Fisheries Exhibition

ANGLING IN GREAT BRITAIN

BY

WILLIAM SENIOR
("RED SPINNER")

AUTHOR OF "WATERSIDE SKETCHES"; "BY STREAM AND SEA";
"TRAVEL AND TROUT IN THE ANTIPODES," &c.

LONDON
1883
WILLIAM CLOWES AND SONS, LIMITED
INTERNATIONAL FISHERIES EXHIBITION
AND 13 CHARING CROSS, S.W.

The following Handbooks upon subjects cognate to the International Fisheries Exhibition are already published, or in active preparation:—

NOW READY.

Demy 8vo., in Illustrated Wrapper 1s. each; or bound in cloth 2s. each.

THE FISHERY LAWS. By FREDERICK POLLOCK, Barrister-at-Law, M.A. (Oxon.), Hon. LL.D. Edin.; Corpus Christi Professor of Jurisprudence in the University of Oxford.

ZOOLOGY AND FOOD FISHES. By GEORGE B. HOWES, Demonstrator of Biology, Normal School of Science, and Royal School of Mines, South Kensington.

BRITISH MARINE AND FRESHWATER FISHES. (*Illustrated.*) By W. SAVILLE KENT, F.L.S., F.Z.S., Author of Official Guide-books to the Brighton, Manchester, and Westminster Aquaria.

APPARATUS FOR FISHING. By E. W. H. HOLDSWORTH, F.L.S., F.Z.S., Special Commissioner for Juries, International Fisheries Exhibition; Author of "Deep Sea Fisheries and Fishing Boats," "British Industries—Sea Fisheries," &c.

THE BRITISH FISH TRADE. By His Excellency SPENCER WALPOLE, Lieut.-Governor of the Isle of Man.

THE UNAPPRECIATED FISHER FOLK. By JAMES G. BERTRAM, Author of "The Harvest of the Sea."

THE SALMON FISHERIES. (*Illustrated.*) By C. E. FRYER. Assistant Inspector of Salmon Fisheries, Home Office.

SEA MONSTERS UNMASKED. (*Illustrated.*) By HENRY LEE, F.L.S.

THE ANGLING CLUBS AND PRESERVATION SOCIETIES OF LONDON AND THE PROVINCES. By J. P. WHEELDON, late Angling Editor of "Bell's Life."

INDIAN FISH AND FISHING. (*Illustrated.*) By FRANCIS DAY, F.L.S., Commissioner for India to International Fisheries Exhibition.

A POPULAR HISTORY OF FISHERIES AND FISHERMEN OF ALL COUNTRIES, FROM THE EARLIEST TIMES. By W. M. ADAMS, B.A., formerly Fellow of New College, Oxford; Author of 'Zenobia: a Tragedy,' and inventor of the Coelometer.

FISH CULTURE. (*Illustrated.*) By FRANCIS DAY, F.L.S., Commissioner for India to International Fisheries Exhibition.

SEA FABLES EXPLAINED. By HENRY LEE, F.L.S. (*Illustrated.*)

ANGLING IN GREAT BRITAIN. By WILLIAM SENIOR ("Red Spinner").

IN THE PRESS.

FISH AS DIET. By W. STEPHEN MITCHELL, M.A. (Cantab.)

EDIBLE CRUSTACEA. By W. SAVILLE KENT, F.L.S., F.Z.S., Author of Official Guidebooks to the Brighton, Manchester, and Westminster Aquaria.

THE LITERATURE OF SEA AND RIVER FISHING. By JOHN J. MANLEY, M.A. (Oxon.)

FOLK LORE OF FISHES: their Place in Fable, Fairy Tale, Myth, and Poetry. By PHIL ROBINSON.

THE OUTCOME OF THE EXHIBITION. By A. J. R. TRENDELL, of the Inner Temple, Barrister-at-Law, Literary Superintendent for the Fisheries Exhibition.

LONDON:
WILLIAM CLOWES AND SONS, LIMITED,
INTERNATIONAL FISHERIES EXHIBITION, & 13, CHARING CROSS.

International Fisheries Exhibition
LONDON, 1883

ANGLING

IN

GREAT BRITAIN

BY

WILLIAM SENIOR

("*RED SPINNER*")

AUTHOR OF "WATERSIDE SKETCHES"; "BY STREAM AND SEA";
"TRAVEL AND TROUT IN THE ANTIPODES," &c.

LONDON
WILLIAM CLOWES AND SONS, Limited
INTERNATIONAL FISHERIES EXHIBITION
AND 13 CHARING CROSS, S.W.
1883

CONTENTS.

CHAP.		PAGE
I.	A General Survey	1
II.	Spring	28
III.	Summer	43
IV.	Autumn	57
V.	Winter	69

ANGLING IN GREAT BRITAIN.

CHAPTER I.

A GENERAL SURVEY.

THE opening sentence of this Handbook I should like to be the expression of a belief—to wit that, take it all in all, year in and year out, there is no better sport in the world for the angler than in Great Britain. The affected sighing after the good old times, and the gloomy apprehension that this highly favoured country is going to the dogs, with which we are all but too familiar, are shared in by him, of course, if he would live up to his privileges; nevertheless, grumbling granted, and too much cause for grumbling granted in the same breath, he has not a great deal to complain of.

At a very interesting meeting last year at the Society of Arts, when a goodly congregation of anglers met to hear and discuss a paper by Mr. Marston on the propagation of coarse fish, we were all highly amused at a speech from an eminent American pisciculturist, who dilated upon the excellent qualities of the Black Bass, and suggested the propriety of introducing that sportive fish into certain British waters. He incidentally referred to some of the angling paragraphs which appear week after week in the English sporting papers, and raised an easy laugh by dwelling upon the fuss sometimes made over infinitesimal catches of fish. Doubtless, there is an element of absurdity in the published reports of an angling contest carried out upon solemnly promulgated rules, and with all the formality of supervision and directions from a responsible committee, yet which results in the gentleman who bears away the most valuable prize winning by an interesting roachlet seven inches long, and a small eel* to make the weight more imposing. Every week, as a matter of fact, if any one cared to search for them, a dozen reports of angling might be selected to support the one-sided view that in this ancient land we are, in the matter of sport, reduced to a very sorry plight.

Since that meeting was held, I have, however, employed myself in carefully noting the corresponding literature of the United States, and I find that the angling records there, where everything is so splendidly new and gloriously big, do not materially differ from our own. Time after time have American sportsmen assured me that the piteous cry, in lamentation for rivers overfished and sport destroyed, is familiar under the Stars and Stripes, and that the American angler has continually to push out to fresh fishing grounds. In New Zealand and Tasmania, where the best trout-fishing in the world will probably be found within a few years, that plaintive wail would also be echoed but for the obvious sparsity of population, and it will be heard when there are more fishermen to worry the fish.

In the angling waters of Great Britain we may at any rate fairly assume that we know the worst. With us, there is no pushing out west until we reach the Rocky Mountain trout. Our sport is confined within a comparatively tiny

* I believe in most angling clubs eels are not recognised as weighable game. But I saw a match won in the manner described.

ring fence of island surf. It is not possible for any angler to explore and discover a new river. But let us be thankful, if we know the worst we also know the best. We know that, by careful conservation, by spread of knowledge upon matters connected with fishes and their food, and by the possibilities of applying to their homes some of the sanitary principles which we are beginning to find out ought not to be neglected by human kind, angling in Great Britain has vastly improved, and may in the future be improved to an almost indefinite extent. There are, no doubt, streams once renowned for their sport, that have been as nearly overfished as any streams can be, and there would be room for despair but for the certainty that the evil can and will be remedied.

If a tenth portion, or a twentieth, of the sound advice given in the Papers and discussions of the International Fisheries Exhibition Conferences, and in the Handbooks published during the summer, were carried out with regard to our lakes and rivers, there would be no necessity to indulge in the unwholesome luxury of sighing after the sleepy old days of our grandmothers. And, in time, theory will have fruition in practice; rivers that are to-day polluted will sparkle clear; trout that are starved, ugly, and unhappy from causes well known *not* to be beyond control, will be as merry as the denizens of the Tennysonian brook; depleted streams will be once more dimpled with rises; and the 'prentice boys may again have the opportunity of protesting against too much salmon, and have that protective clause (purely imaginary, there is every reason to believe), of which so much has been written, inserted in their indentures.

In confirmation of the humble belief which is expressed at the beginning of this chapter, let me proceed to the recital of a few facts. A deceased statesman, who was himself extremely fond of felling his opponents with statistics, once, when such tough arguments went against him, contemptuously remarked that figures might be made to prove anything. My figures, I hope, will prove simply what they are intended to show, namely, that angling in Great Britain, up to the present moment, is anything but a played-out institution.

In the very last month of the present season some magnificent takes of salmon have been recorded from nearly all the Scotch rivers. The largest fish appears to have been taken on the Stobhall water, of the Tay, by Lord Ruthven. It weighed 54 lbs., and was of such fine proportions that it was reserved for preservation and setting up in the museum of the Perthshire Society of Natural Science. This, it is said, was not only the heaviest fish killed by the rod in the Tay during the season, but the heaviest since 1870, when a gentleman, on the Stanley Waters, killed a fish of 61 lbs. In one day upon the Stobhall water, thirty-four salmon were killed: and on the following day two rods landed two-and-twenty fish.

In the Tweed and Teviot the anglers also obtained sport, sometimes three, sometimes four, and in one instance Col. Vivian and Mr. Arkwright, on the Rutherford Water, killed nearly a dozen fish. On the Mertoun Water the Hon. H. Brougham had twelve fish, and on the Earl of Home's water (Bingham), a couple of gentlemen used their rods to some purpose, the result of a day's sport being fish of 24 lbs., 23 lbs., 23 lbs., 21 lbs., 16 lbs., 16 lbs., 11 lbs., 11 lbs., 8 lbs., and 6 lbs. In another part of the river, a day or two later, Mr. Brougham killed thirteen fish, and on the Floors' Water the Duke of Roxburghe, in one afternoon, had four—one of 22 lbs., another of 12 lbs., and two of 10 lbs. Up to the 11th November in the season of 1881 (the Tweed close time being from December 1st to January 31st), I read somewhere that one gentleman at one stand had killed 3,782 lbs. of salmon; while a few days after, 177½ lbs. fell to his rod in a single day, with nine fish. The same angler, in one day, in the next season, took nine fish weighing respectively 25 lbs., 25 lbs., 23 lbs., 19½ lbs., 16½ lbs., 16 lbs., 16 lbs., 14 lbs., 15 lbs.—total, 170 lbs.

The finest sport, probably, in this present season of 1883, was that on the Spey, which, after the removal of the nets, began to afford the rodsters a round of splendid sport. According to a report in the *Field*, from which paper I have also taken the figures of this year's Tweed fishing, General Gipps, on the 1st of October, landed seven; on the 2nd, five; on the 3rd, three; on the 4th, seven; on the 5th, five; and on the 6th three salmon. On another water, Mr. Todd killed seven fish; on the 2nd October, six; on the 3rd, six; and on the 4th, six. On the Gordon Castle Water the Duke of Richmond, the Earl of March, Lord Francis Gordon Lennox, Lady Florence Gordon Lennox, and several visitors every day made most enviable baskets. It is unnecessary to go through all the daily returns in the early part of October, but taking one day I find that the Duke of Richmond to his own rod had six salmon, weighing respectively 27 lbs., 24 lbs., 22½ lbs., 22 lbs., 20 lbs., and 19 lbs., besides a brace of grilse weighing 8 and 10 lbs. respectively. On another day His Grace got a 30 lbs. and a 20 lbs. salmon; and, on the same day, the Earl of March killed six fish—of 24 lbs., 19 lbs., 15 lbs., 21 lbs., 21 lbs., and 12½ lbs. On another day the noble earl must have been kept pretty well occupied with his seven salmon—of 15 lbs., 15 lbs., 17 lbs., 17 lbs., 16 lbs., 18 lbs., and 22 lbs., and four grilse, three of 10 lbs. and one of 9 lbs. Even a bishop who was fishing the Water (St. Alban's) got his three salmon and one grilse, while several ladies were quite as successful.

In another part of the country I read that on the Aboyne section of the Dee a gentleman, in one day, killed his eight salmon—from 8 lbs. to 37 lbs., and on the following day, with the natural minnow, he had four, the largest of which was 30 lbs. These returns are taken from one paper only, the *Field*, of October 13th, and they tell of sport that should surely satisfy the most rapacious sportsman. At the same time they convincingly indicate that while such fishing is to be had at home, there is no need to fly to foreign parts, even to try conclusions in the swarming rivers of Canada.

As to trout fishing, I do not happen to have on hand a suitable clipping from which to quote, but I can draw upon a recent experience of my own to supply all that is necessary for my argument. Within thirty miles of London, which I did not leave till eleven o'clock in the morning, I killed, mostly with a small alder fly, on one summer's day, ten brace of trout. The largest, it is true, was a very ugly fish of two pounds and a quarter, but the rest were beyond reproach, and ranged between a pound and a half and half a pound. This, I may be told by some friendly monitor, is nothing to boast about. Nor is it. But it is quite enough to satisfy my wants, and, indeed, the more modest basket of four brace and a half, which on my very last outing in August rewarded seven hours' hard whipping, made me as happy and contented as a man has a right to be in this vale of tears.

The business transacted with the Thames trout appeared in an authentic return prepared by Mr. W. H. Brougham, the Secretary of the Thames Angling Preservation Society, in the summer. He gave the following captures as representing one week's Thames trouting between Chertsey Weir and Kingston only :—Chertsey Weir, four fish, weighing respectively 7¾ lbs., 4 lbs. 14 oz., 5 lbs., and 3¼ lbs. ; Shepperton Weir, four fish, weighing respectively 5¼ lbs., 4½ lbs., 3¾ lbs., and 2 lbs. ; Sunbury Weir, two fish, weighing respectively 7 lbs., and 4½ lbs. ; opposite the Waterworks Sunbury, one fish weighing 10 lbs. ; Hampton Court Weir four fish, weighing respectively 14 lbs. 10 oz., 7 lbs., 4 lbs., and 2 lbs. ; Thames Ditton, one fish, weighing 7 lbs. 2 oz. ; Kingston, one fish, weighing 7 lbs. Thus we have a total of seventeen fish, weighing together 99 lbs. 14 oz.

The coarse fish have also been kind enough to furnish me with ready examples of the quality of our English sport. Mr. Jardine, who is accepted as the most successful pike angler of the country, as the superb specimens shown by him in the western arcade at the Fisheries Exhibition will indicate, is thus spoken of in a newspaper paragraph :—" Messrs. A. Jardine and Knechtli had a magnificent catch of pike the other day, which were shown at the Gresham Angling Society. Ten fish weighed in the society's scales 135 lbs. This represented two days' fishing. This capture has no parallel in angling history, so far as London clubs are concerned, because the fish shown were only the largest, and they took thirty more, from 3 lbs. to 7 lbs."

In *Bell's Life* of January 7, 1883, I read—" We have seen or heard of some remarkable takes of pike and perch recently. One of the finest shows of pike to be seen this season was that of Mr. H. D. Hughes, jun., last Saturday. Fishing with his brother in a private lake, the united take was forty good fish. The largest, weighing 25 lbs., was caught on single gut, and was on view last Monday at Messrs. Alfred and Son's, Moorgate Street. Equally remarkable was another day's sport. Mr. Carter Milburn, fishing last week in private water (a lake), took, between eight and ten o'clock on the morning of Thursday, six pike weighing 20 lbs., 17 lbs., 15 lbs., 11 lbs., and 6 lbs. This achievement is all the more remarkable when we know that Mr. Milburn has been for years deprived of his left arm. The business was managed entirely with the snap-tackle."

Perch exist in such incredible quantities in many British waters, that we might almost pass them by, and take them, like official reports, as read. In the *Field* of August 25, however, an account appeared of the capture by two anglers, between eleven and five o'clock, in Slapton Ley, of more than 800 fish. This haul was made on a well-known piece of water which may be fished by all comers on payment of a small fee. The accuracy of the statement was questioned, but the evidence of subsequent correspondents confirmed it, one gentleman stating that he and a friend in five hours fishing took 476 perch.

What may be done amongst roach and barbel was duly set forth in the Paper on Freshwater Fishing read at one of the Exhibition conferences by Mr. Wheeldon. In the short space of five hours on a winter day, he killed, in the Hampshire Avon—a notable roach river from Ringwood upwards —75 lbs. of roach, numbers of which were considerably over a pound in weight. In another portion of his Paper he stated that he and Mr. Smurthwaite not long ago killed three hundredweight of barbel in one day, near Sonning Weir. In the tidal waters of the Thames during this present autumn, takes of dace of 35 lbs., 26 lbs., and 25 lbs. have been registered by the Richmond and Twickenham punts-men. During the month of July, according to the *Fishing Gazette*, in a lake near Swindon, open on payment to the public, Messrs. Wheatstone and Walker, of the Stanley Anglers' Club, caught 230 lbs. of tench in five days. One of these anglers, on July 9th, took with rod and line twenty-five fish, nine being over 4 lbs., nine over 3 lbs., and seven over 2 lbs.. The total weight of the days' angling was 89½ lbs.

These results, which speak for themselves, I give as they occur to me at the moment, and not by any effort at research. They fairly enough serve the purpose I have in view, and if I wished to extend the list of good baskets, the averages of the last five years, as they may be unearthed from the periodical literature devoted to the subject, would probably show as fine, and much finer sport in some of the branches of angling upon which I have casually touched.

But the rapidly increased and increasing number of anglers in Great Britain should be a continual stimulus to exertion in keeping up the stock of fresh-water fish. Such an impetus has been given to the culture of Salmonidæ of all descriptions (adding latterly to the fish indigenous to British waters, the brook trout of North America), that there is little fear that they will be neglected.

Private fish-hatching establishments have sprung up in England as well as in Scotland, from which our colonial rivers are being tenanted, and by which losses and deterioration at home may be made good at any time; and the interesting collection of fish cultural appliances at the Exhibition must have been, to hosts of observers during the summer, a serviceable object lesson that cannot fail to produce practical results in time to come.

The increase of anglers, however—and this is a point we are too apt to overlook in considering the general question

—has been chiefly amongst the classes of the population that cannot afford, either in time or money, to fish the best waters for the best fish. The anglers who devote themselves to salmon and trout can, in the main, look very well after themselves. Give them an adequate legislation that shall ensure fair play against the proprietors and occupiers to whom the netting of salmon is a business, and all other things will, without much trouble, be added unto them. They represent the higher branches of the sport of angling. They are the followers of Cotton rather than Father Izaak, the patron saint of what are termed general anglers; and the time has gone by when the humble angler, who is content with a modest day's roach or perch-fishing, is regarded by them with contemptuous indifference. The angling-books of twenty years ago show that the fortunate individuals who could betake themselves to Norway, or across the St. George's Channel, or North of the Tweed, were given to looking down from a lofty pedestal upon their less fortunate brother sportsman, who was dubbed a Cockney, and held up, together with his floats, worms, maggots, and ground-bait, to derision. But that day is past.

If space permitted, it would be interesting to trace how the change has been brought about. Broadly speaking, it has been done by the printing-press, and during the last twenty years, not so much by angling-books, as by literature of a more unsubstantial character. The journalistic fathers in Israel are answerable primarily for the tens of thousands of members of angling clubs, who weekly obtain healthful recreation by the waterside. "Ephemera" aforetime of *Bell's Life*, Francis Francis, Greville, F., and Cholmondeley Pennell (too young to be a veteran yet, but still ancient enough as an angling writer to come within the category), by their contributions to journals and magazines awakened popular interest; and it happened that a revolution in the means of communication had come at an opportune time, to add to their teachings the necessary opportunities of putting them into practice. Anglers have now an organ of their own in the *Fishing Gazette;* Mundella's Act was passed for the especial behoof of bottom-fishers; railway companies are recognizing the brotherhood as of sufficient influence to be considered in the granting of special privileges; and the Fish Culture Association, of which the Marquis of Exeter is President, would never have been started, had not the necessity been felt of looking after the stock of coarse-fish in rivers frequented by the many. It must suffice, however, to take these things for granted, and so I pass on with the hearty wish that all societies, and all movements which aim at assisting and encouraging the fair general angler, may prosper abundantly. The man who is a fair fisherman, though his ambition soar no higher than a plate of gudgeon from the well-raked gravel, has his place in the common confraternity, and is deserving of consideration.

The general angler at the present time is not altogether without his apprehensions. Angling Associations have befriended him, but the awakened interest which he has himself helped to extend, threatens to curtail his privileges. Claims to the ownership of waters hitherto considered public are being advanced with the view of keeping him at a distance. As, however, the Defence Associations should be able to prevent wrong-handed or high-handed proceedings, this, though a vexatious sign of the times, is a difficulty that will be removed, one way or another, by appeal to the law. Still, it should be mentioned in a general survey of the English angler's present position. I confess I see most cause for alarm in the snapping-up of every available bit of water by societies of gentlemen who can afford to pay for it. For this there is no help. We live in a free country, and if the owner of a stream, which his forefathers permitted to be fished by his neighbours, chooses to let it at a rental, he has the right to do so. Equally have a dozen city gentlemen, who love the amusement of angling, and can, by their purses, command the means of indulging in it under agreeable conditions, the right, morally and legally, of securing it for a consideration, or without one if they have the chance. Nevertheless, the effect is to limit the waters available to the masses of anglers.

The larger rivers beloved of general anglers are open, under easy and equitable regulations. The Thames, Trent, Ouse, and others of that class, are not yet parcelled out into subscription waters, and of smaller streams, like the Lea, and portions of the Colne, it should not be forgotten that the small fee demanded for a day-ticket is more than counterbalanced by the advantages gained by watching and preservation. In the immediate vicinity of large towns, indeed, there is something to be said for the oft-heard complaint that open waters are scarcely worth fishing, unless they are under the charge of some such model guardians as the Thames Angling Preservation Society. The cutting down of ancient privileges is suffered mostly in rural or semi-rural districts, to which town anglers were wont to issue, attracted as much by the pleasures of the country surroundings, as the more direct operations of fish capture.

Of the joys of angling I have nothing at present to say, except to remark that it is a sport which, more than any other, owes much of its fascination to features that are only indirectly connected with it. Some years ago a masterly essay (by its editor) appeared in the *New Quarterly* upon trout fishing, and this sentence at once challenged my attention: "One apologist will talk of wandering amid pleasant scenery, rod in hand. The hypocrite! As if the scenery were the inducement, and not the rod, which he affects to speak of so lightly. The best of all apologies is Shakespeare's, and yet it is a poor one :—

> 'The pleasant'st angling is to see the fish
> Cut, with her golden oars, the silver stream,
> And greedily devour the treacherous bait.'"

In a couple of angling books which I had at that time cast upon the waters, I had endeavoured to remind the reader of the countless charms to be found in the lanes and hedgerows through which, on an angling excursion, we pass to the cornfield; and the objects of interest visible from the footpath amongst the waving grain; and the meadows "painted with delight" over which we brush through the grass to the river's brink; to say nothing of the harvest which the eye may gather in the intervals of fishing. Wherefore I began to hold court of justice upon myself, if haply it were true, after all, that we were indeed the hypocrites thus described. The verdict was one of "Not Guilty," and much was I comforted upon taking up the magazine, in fear and trembling as to what would follow, to find the accusing article itself flavoured with a very pretty sprinkling of poetry and sentiment. All in sweet form came the fine summer day, and the rill trickling down the remote hillside " among club rushes and the blue water-grasses, till it reaches the valley, finding its way along, a mere thread, half lost to sight at times beneath the herbage, then stagnating for a space into a little pool," &c. It was my turn now. "The hypocrite!

mused I. "As if he climbed the hillside to catch trout in the thread-like trickle!"

The old names by which the pastime of angling is known are, it will be noticed, significant on this head. It is "The Gentle Craft," and "The Contemplative Man's Recreation." To be sure, there are plenty of anglers of all ranks who are pot-hunters pure and simple. They take their surly way to the water, doggedly settle down to slay, and are deaf and blind to the compensations which Nature, in her kindlier mood, offers against that too frequent ill-luck for which the angler in Great Britain, in Greater Britain, and all the world over, must be prepared. But the rule is otherwise; the majority of anglers in this country, at all events, *do* take appreciative note of the scenery; *do* keep a friendly eye upon bird, beast, and insect; *do* delight in the foliage of the coppice, the whispering of the sedges, and the long gay procession of flowers, even from the curious blossom of the coltsfoot, which is probably the first to greet him in the earliest spring days, to the yellow stars of the solitary ragwort, which shivers in the late October days.

It stands to reason that it should be so. Amongst out-of-door sportsmen the angler is peculiar. The deer-stalker has little to look at but barren hills misnamed a forest, or the broad sky above him; the fox-hunter has his horse and his own neck to study, and the briskness of impetuous advance to divert his thoughts; the fowler's eye has a definite duty to perform. The angler, if using a fly-rod, has frequently-recurring "waits," what time he moves from stream to stream; the bottom-fisher, too, has a superfluity of enforced leisure at his disposal. And over and above all the British angler lives in a country whose rural parts are unique in their winsomeness. Walton's famous old book savours of honeysuckles, hawthorn hedges, sycamore trees, and crystal streams. He was a typical angler, and the type remains.

We may now pass to a more practical branch of our general survey, and having glanced at some of the characteristics of the situation as concerning the angler, may take a birdseye view of the inland waters of Great Britain. I do not, however, pretend to attempt anything like a guide to the rivers, nor even to furnish a comprehensive list. *The Angler's Diary* deals in brief with all the fishing districts of the United Kingdom, and, indeed, of the world, so far as they are known, and to that useful little book shall the inquiring reader be referred. All that I am able to do is to hint at the main features of our chief angling resorts.

A bulky handbook might, for example, be written upon the one section comprising the lochs and rivers of the

> "Land of brown heath and shaggy wood,
> Land of the mountain and the flood."

Placing, as is but meet, the migratory Salmonidæ at the top of the list, Scotland naturally first claims our notice. To the ordinary angler, however, all but a few of the prime waters, which are a source of rich revenue to Scotland, are close boroughs. The fishings, like the shootings, are rented at enormous figures, although there are, here and there, given to the sojourner at particular hotels, the privilege of wetting his line in odd reaches of well-known salmon rivers. There is never so much difficulty in obtaining permission to fish for *Salmo fario*, or, as our Scotch friends call it, the yellow trout, and if some travellers complain of persistent refusals to applications for permission, I must personally say that I have always had reason to be grateful for ready kindness in various parts of the country.

On the whole, the angler visiting Scotland cannot do better than take his technical instructions about salmon fishing from Francis Francis's 'Book on Angling.' Perhaps no English angler has had more experience of the Scotch rivers, from the angler's point of view, than he. It is no secret to the initiated that the list of salmon and sea-trout flies, which he gives for the various rivers and lakes of Scotland, Ireland, and Wales, cost him years of labour, and that in compiling them he received the assistance of some of the most experienced of British anglers.

What the principal Scotch rivers produce I have already illustrated by figures. The Tweed is held in high esteem as an angling river, though it is not so long, and does not form so large a watershed as the Tay. The Kirkcudbrightshire Dee, the Cree, and the Luce, are small rivers in the south of Scotland, and the Annan and Nith, the former famous for its sea-trout and herling, also run into the Solway Firth. The Tay is a superb salmon river, and like the Tweed has, in its lower part, to be commanded from a boat. It yields, with its many tributaries, good spring fishing. Aberdeenshire is a famous county for the angler, for it can boast of its Dee and Don, and a number of smaller streams. Inverness, also, is a notable angling county, containing as it does the magnificent Spey. This river has peculiar characteristics for the angler, having high banks and much rough, rapid water, demanding the exercise of all his skill. In this county is also the Ness, where the public have access on given days to a portion of the water near the Highland capital. In the Beauly, some years ago, Lord Louth killed to his own rod 146 salmon in five days, and this beautiful river is still first-rate for fish.

Upon the Thurso, in the extreme north, the fishing opens earlier than in any other portion of the United Kingdom.

Argyllshire, the country of the Mac Callum More, has, in addition to its lochs, a number of small salmon rivers, such as the Awe, the Orchy, and the Leven. In Banffshire the best salmon rivers are the Deveron and Fiddich. In Berwickshire are the Blackadder and the Whitadder, two good trouting streams. The Findhorn, once a phenomenal salmon river, is in Elginshire, and it is on record that years ago 360 salmon were caught in the same pool in one day. This, however, was exceeded by another miraculous draught of fishes described by the Earl of Moray, who wrote to his countess that 1,300 salmon had been taken in a night. There is fair fishing occasionally even now in the Findhorn, but ruthless nettings below have considerably spoiled it. The Lossie, in the same county, is good for sea-trout and yellow trout. Forfarshire has the North and South Esk. The Clyde, whose falls are fatal to the ascent of salmon, is in its upper waters excellent for trout, and it is of additional interest to anglers since the experiment of introducing grayling into Scotland has there been successfully carried out. The best rivers of Perthshire are the Garry, the Tummel, the Lyon, the peerless Tay already referred to, and the Teith. Roxburghshire, besides the Tweed, which is famous for both trout and salmon, many of its casts being historical, and which has romantic historical associations with Melrose, Dryburgh, Norham, and Kelso, has also the Teviot, which, like the Ale, the Bowmont, the Jed, the Kale, the Rule, and other such minor streams, are of excellent repute for trout. Sutherlandshire, the paradise of loch fishers and the stronghold of the *Salmo ferox*, has the Brora, an early salmon river, where the fish run large; the Borgie, excellent for grilse and sea-trout; the Inver, where the wandering angler staying at Loch Inver can fish, for a daily payment; the Lexford, a short river, but that still is the second best salmon river in the county, and the Shin one of the best rivers in the Highlands.

As for the lochs, one might almost be pardoned for using the familiar expression that their name is legion. Loch Lomond, between Dumbarton and Stirlingshire; Loch Awe, in Argyllshire; Lochs Tay, Rannoch, Earn, and Katrine, in Perthshire; Lochs Ness, Lochie, and Lagan, Inverness-shire; Lochs Maree, Luichart, and Fannich, in Ross-shire, at once occur to us; while below the Grampians there are Loch Leven, with its wonderful fishing, and St. Mary's Loch in the Yarrow country. Some of these grand sheets of water contain the destructive pike, and perch, which are only less fatal to trout by reason of their smaller size. But in the hundreds of lochs which lie twinkling within the hollows of the bonny Scotch mountains there is an abundance of small trout, and heavy specimens of the *Salmo fario,* while many are inhabited by the great lake trout, the night prowler that so seldom takes a fly, and to which the name of *ferox* has been aptly given.

Ireland is not so much patronised by English anglers as Scotland, though there is more and cheaper general sport at his command. The Green Island, manifold as are its physical beauties and angling capabilities, has been not a little neglected. Of late years there has been some excuse, perhaps, for timorous tourists, though surely never was fear more ungrounded; but to the angler, for some incomprehensible reason, Ireland has never been such an attraction as Scotland, though, as I have hinted, a stranger who can only afford to expend a moderate amount of money in his amusements, and desires a variety of fishing, would do much better in Ireland than in Scotland. The largest pike in Europe, I believe, are roaming in the depths of the big lakes; it is the land *par excellence* of the white trout;

and all round the coast, from the merry but much preserved Bush, within easy hail of Giant's Causeway, to the early Lee, in county Cork, the salmon come and go with beautiful regularity. One of the most delightful angling tours I ever had was in Ireland, fishing my journey from Sligo through Connemara to Galway by easy stages, and taking whatever came in my way—perch, pike, brown trout, white trout, and salmon—with praiseworthy impartiality. Rivers, mountains, land and sea, the courteous people, even the pigs and wretched hovels—everything, in short, but the too freely weeping skies, contributed to the sum total of a pleasant holiday.

The angling in Ireland, though very good, is not what it was when the chapters of 'Wild Sports of the West' were written. The fish are, generally speaking, of the same class as those to be found in the Scotch rivers—salmon and trout everywhere, and in the larger lakes leviathan pike, and here and there bream. There are gillaroo in Lough Erne, and pollan in Lough Neagh. It goes without saying in these days, when the taste for angling has extended so much, that the free fishings are not numerous.

Still there are many bits of open salmon fishing, and lakes that are to all intents and purposes free; and the sea and brown trout fishing is plentiful enough to satisfy the most rapacious appetite. Boats are cheap and the boatmen very modest in their demands, and what is more, the latter are always satisfied with the treatment they receive, while their humorous sayings and doings are a source of continual amusement. One salmon fishing licence will do for the whole of Ireland, which is a great advantage. The open season, as elsewhere, is from February 2nd to October 31st, with the usual exceptions of special districts. The principal rivers in the south are the Blackwater, the Lee, and the Bandon, while upon the wild shores of Bantry Bay and by Glengariff there are plenty of trout streams. Close by, in county Kerry, there are the Killarney lakes, overrun during periods of the year by tourists, spoiled by the use of cross lines, but still, in early months, not hopeless for the rodster.

Continuing our way up the western coast, we come to the estuary of the magnificent river Shannon, which contains samples of most of the fish to be found in Ireland. Songs have been sung in praise of the salmon of this river, and it has obtained more prominence in the literature of sport than any other Irish river, which is but natural, seeing that it runs from Leitrim in the north, passing through a number of lakes, the last of which is the prolific fishing ground of Lough Derg. County Clare, being somewhat out of the way, and not much written or talked about, is but little frequented by anglers, but the best pike fishing in Ireland is probably to be obtained in some of its lakes.

Galway, according to its angling value, should have been mentioned first. In this county is the famous fishery of Ballynahinch, the white trout station of Glendalough, and the Galway river, in which the salmon fishery has been brought to a high pitch of perfection; it drains Corrib and Mask, in the latter of which trout of the phenomenal proportions of twenty pounds are very occasionally taken.

From Galway the angling tourist makes his way through Connemara by Westport to Ballina, a famous centre on the Moy, with Lough Conn not far distant. Mayo is the country of which Maxwell wrote, and there are privileges in connection with its fisheries that make this station the most attractive of all for the man of moderate means, though the upper portions of the Moy are strictly preserved. Lough Arrow is in the next county, Sligo, but the best fishing is in the river which runs from Lough Gill through the county town

Still further north, in wild and beautiful Donegal, we have on the southern boundary of the county the river Erne, with the grand lough of that name stretching down by Enniskillen into Fermanagh. The short length of water between Lough Erne and Ballyshannon used to be, and, for aught I know to the contrary, now is, one of the favourite salmon reaches in the country; and hard by, in Leitrim, we have the Bundrowes river and Lough Melvin, in which some good fish, at reasonable charges, may be obtained, especially during April and May. Across, in the other corner of Ulster, there is the Bann, with Lough Neagh. These are the principal angling resorts in the sister island; but we should not forget the Blackwater, the Suir, the Slaney, and the pretty trout streams within convenient distance of Dublin. As a rule, it may be taken that the angler, more particularly the angler who will be satisfied with sea-trout, brown trout, occasionally gillaroo, and lively pike fishing, can never very well do wrong in going to Ireland.

The principality of Wales is a delightful country for the trout angler who will be as a rule content with small fish, and who can make up for the rest with the most picturesque and beautiful scenery. In North Wales the principal rivers are the Conway (good occasionally for salmon), the Dee, the Dovey, the higher waters of the Severn, the Clwyd, and the Verniew; while in South Wales, where the sewin gives spirited sport in the autumn, and the brown trout run to a larger size than in the small lakes and mountain streams of the north country, we have the Ogmore, Taff, Taw, Teme, Towy, Usk, Monnow, and Wye. The salmon fishing of the Usk is proverbial, and I have in my possession a photograph given to me by the late Mr. Crawshay, of Cyfarthfa Castle, at the close of a day's successful trout fishing, during a frosty day in the month of February a few years ago, representing nine salmon killed by him on October 22nd, 1874, with the fly; and a singular thing in connection with this day's sport was that the three largest fish, one of 22 lbs., one of 19 lbs., and one of 16 lbs., were hooked foul, the salmon being, as they too often are, in a more playful than feeding humour; yet carried their gambols too far, and were nicked accordingly—two in the pectoral fin, and a third in the side. These fish were placed upon an unhinged door, which was tilted up by a couple of men to allow Mr. Crawshay, who was a very skilful amateur photographer, to take their likenesses.

Considering the amount of poaching to which the English rivers, up to within ten or fifteen years, were subjected, and the gross neglect from which they long suffered, it is marvellous that in all parts of the country the commoner kinds of fishing should be so good as they are at the present time; and considering the number of anglers who test their value upon every available day of the year, it would not be surprising if the rule was to toil all day and catch nothing, and if the language of every English angler was that of the prophet of old, "The fishers also shall mourn, and all they that cast angle into the brooks." But, as I have remarked on a previous page, we have more to be thankful for than to complain of.

It would be invidious to single out one county as better than another, were it not that our best trouting districts are limited. There is probably no county in England that has not a trout stream of some kind; and tributary streams and brooklets known only to a few, and very naturally kept secret by them, sometimes keep up very ample stores of surreptitious trout. But the true trouting counties are comparatively few. Beginning with the south, Cornwall may be passed by with a brief reference, although all the streams trickling down from the backbone of the hills which constitute the Cornish highlands, contain more or less of trout. Devonshire is quite another matter. Its larger trout rivers are numerous, and salmon are taken in Taw and Torridge, in Exe and Tavy, while the interior is intersected in all directions with lively little streams. There are a few strictly preserved trout streams in Dorsetshire, and a good salmon river in the Stour, which joins itself with the Avon at Christchurch, the Avon itself being swelled by a famous grayling river, the Wiley, from the Salisbury Plain region.

The largest river in Great Britain, and the one to which most importance is attached by the main body of general anglers, is, of course, the Thames, with its magnificent watershed representing a basin of over six thousand miles. It is not so long as the Severn by some twenty odd miles, but it is fed by a rich array of tributaries right and left. In its higher portions, under the influence of the Cotswold hills, there are the Windrush and Coln, both capital trout streams. In the Kennet, the most important of its southern tributaries, the richest specimens to be found in England of the *Salmo fario* are taken. To all London anglers the Roden, the Lea, the Colne, Wick, and Thame are familiar, while the trout and trout fishing of the Wandle and Darenth, the one on the west and the other on the east side of southern London, but both almost within hearing of the roar of its traffic, are traditional. In the midlands there are the brilliant Derbyshire streams, which may be considered midway, in physical characteristics, between the pastoral rivers of the Hampshire lowlands (the Itchen and the Test) and the mountain burns of Wales and Scotland.

The Derbyshire streams, being for the most part open to the purchasers of day tickets, are a good deal fished, but there are plenty of respectable trout and grayling yet to be taken, and the anglers of the big cities—London in the south, and Manchester and Liverpool in the north—have in them splendid opportunities of exercising the art of fly-fishing from spring, to the close of the grayling season, when spring comes again. The Derwent, Wye, and the Dove rising in the mountains that characterise the peak country, are tributaries of the Trent, from which a few salmon are taken, and which affords everlasting sport to the Nottingham anglers, who have founded a school of their own, and whose reserves of coarse fish seem to be little affected by the contributions levied upon them. A kindred river to the Trent, though running in a southerly instead of a northerly direction, and delivering its tribute, like the Trent, into the Humber, is the Yorkshire Ouse, into which, galloping down from the Pennine chain, are delivered a succession of first-rate trout and grayling streams, the Swale, the Yore, the Nid, and the Wharfe; and on the other side, easily commanded from Scarborough, and in its earlier waters running under the north wolds, is the Yorkshire Derwent, the grayling fishing of which is not inferior to that of the Wharfe.

Lancashire, in days long since passed, was probably an excellent angling county throughout, but the Mersey and the Irwell have been years ago pressed into the service of manufacture and commerce, and we have to go into north Lancashire to the Ribble, Lune, Hodder, and the waters of Ribblesdale, before anything like adequate sport can be obtained. The lakes of Cumberland, and its fine river the

Eden, still maintain their long-established character; and on the other side of the country, the north and south Tyne have not entirely lost their salmon, and certainly not their trout. Above Newcastle, the Wansbeck, the Coquet, Breamish and Till, keep up the reputation of the border streams for trout angling. The Severn I have not passed by intentionally. But it is as much a Welsh as an English stream, having a decidedly Welsh origin, and by its tributaries watering a good deal of Welsh country. At any rate, I do not mention it last because it is least, for we have to thank the Severn for some of the unsurpassed grayling rivers of Worcestershire and Herefordshire. The Teme and the Arrow, with the Lugg, a tributary of the Wye, are not second to those of any part of England for the quality and quantity of their grayling. On the eastern coast of England, other than the trout streams of the border, there are some coarse fish rivers in Essex and Suffolk, and three particularly good general angling streams, namely, the Ouse (Bedfordshire and Huntingdonshire), which is famous for its bream and pike, the Nen, and Welland. In east Anglia there is a special description of angling, to which reference will be made in another portion of this pamphlet, while beyond the Wash there is the fen country, with the Ancholme and Witham; upon these the Sheffield anglers swoop in their hundreds, and, when fishing matches are arranged, by their thousands, during the summer season, and, spite of the rows of rods, uncommonly good baskets are occasionally taken away.

The angling of England is more prosaic, taking it as a whole, than in either of the other countries that compose the national union. Until we get considerably north of the Trent, and within measurable distance of the lakes and mountains of Cumberland, our landscape scenery is softly pleasing rather than imposingly wild and romantic. Our rivers for the most part flow tranquilly through fat meadows, upon which the mildest mannered kine graze their fill. They are at every turn brought under tribute by the millowner, sometimes becoming hopelessly demoralised as a reward for the service they render. They do not thunder through gloomy granite gorge as, in some portion of their career, do the rivers of Scotland. With impetuous torrent they do not dash around massive boulders, as do well-remembered Irish salmon streams. They *flow* to the sea, seldom leaping, or boiling, or swirling, after the manner of rivers cradled in mountain heights.

Thanks, however, to the liberally distributed tributaries, and the drainage of the hill countries, the English angler has, in the wide variety of waters from which he may take his choice when meditating a piscatorial excursion, the opportunity of forming acquaintance with many a bright, swift-running river, making music in such solitary dales as those of Derbyshire, or amongst the rocky walls and overhanging foliage characterising many of the Devonshire streams. There is, in short, some sort of angling in every part of the country. Even the Isle of Wight has a trout stream if the tourist only knew it, and the trout of the Isle of Man have certainly outlived the animal which is the sign manual of the Manxman.

In an essay of this description the writer is confronted with the difficulty of deciding how to act, without dwelling too much or too little upon any one subject. Clearly the orthodox method of dealing with the many-sided topic of angling will not answer. Space would altogether fail me to deal in detail with the various methods of angling, or with the thousand-and-one appliances which are recommended for the successful prosecution of the art, and which have of late multiplied to a bewildering extent. I have already declined the duties of guide to localities, and in the same spirit I must put aside the pleasant functions of tutor in the rudiments. Nor would such a *rôle* be necessary even if it were expedient. There is nothing new to be said about practical angling, after such past masters as Francis Francis, Stewart, Stoddart, Cholmondeley Pennell, Manley, Greville F., Keene, Foster, Alfred, Martin, and others too numerous to mention have had their say.

Easy, therefore, is my conscience in shaking off the temptations which have beset me to attempt a technical disquisition upon the best method of tying a fly, making and fitting up rod and line, handling it from bank or boat, impaling a worm, or compounding ground bait, except so far as may point a moral or adorn a tale. These are most essential subjects to study and master let no man gainsay, but I will courteously ask the reader to permit me to deal with the subject, in what space remains, in the spirit—if I may employ the expression—rather than in the letter. This, after not a little cogitation, I have resolved to do by endeavouring, so far as in me lies, to conduct the reader through the Angler's Year, making spring, summer, autumn and winter develop the essential types of angling in Great Britain.

CHAPTER II.

SPRING.

THE boundary lines between the seasons, into which we will take the liberty of separating the angler's year, must for our present purposes be somewhat more elastic than those of the calendar. At the very beginning, for example, we shall find it convenient to assume that spring begins in February, for in that month both salmon and trout anglers have a legal right to commence operations; and we are bound by all considerations of honour and tradition to deal with them in the forefront. There is no British freshwater fish absolutely out of season in February. On the contrary, some of the coarse fish—a designation which, spite of its unsatisfactory character, we may continue to use for want of a better—are at this period in good condition, more particularly if winter continues to have a firm grip upon the infant year. It sometimes, but of late rarely, happens that February is a tolerably pleasant month, and in that case general angling is prosecuted with the ardour which comes of knowing that the fence months are hurrying on apace. The coarse fish just now, however, must bide their time, and be content with swimming about in other chapters.

Besides, who would forgive the heretic who suggested a thought of the common herd, while the kings and princes of our watery realm were at hand? It is a moot point with many anglers whether salmon or trout fishing be the highest order of sport. For myself, I hold the salmon to be the king of fish, but trouting to be the choicest form of angling; in the word salmon, including all the migratory species, and by trouting meaning also **fly-fishing** for grayling. This predilection for the trout rod is a whim of my own, I am aware, in which few will probably give me countenance. At the same time, there are foolish folks of some experience on lake and river who take a like view, and I mention the matter here to justify the statement that the point with some is an open one. But there can be no question that salmon and trout between them represent the science, ethics, poetry, rhetoric (and all the rest) of the delicious sport of angling.

Had every salmon-fisher a record to show like some of those transcribed in the preceding chapter, he might sing everlasting anthems in praise of that phase of angling. We should then all be salmon fishers according to our opportunities. But it is weary work toiling through the day with one "fish" as a result, and as often as not with nothing to show for the pains. That day, in the first weeks of the season, will probably be cold and wet and blustering, and the play uncommonly like downright hard work. Still the big rod is plied, the long cast essayed upon every likely pool, the fly changed (changed too often by some men), and every tactic observed. The angler loves his work, and when it runs in the direction of salmon there are many special breezes that keep his zeal alive. A coterie of anglers lounging round the smoking-room fire after a day's fishing, betray in a very brief conversation why they will not stoop to any but salmon angling.

The things we do *not* know about a salmon, for instance, would make, if not a book, a pamphlet of decent dimensions. How the noble *salar* spends his time at sea, and his tastes in the item of food, if any, are discussed. Fishing men are never tired of propounding, as a sort of conundrum, the question, "Why do salmon take a fly?" And after long years echo answers, "Why?" Next comes the unpleasant subject of *Saprolegnia ferax*, and then the conversation surely drifts down to those lower proprietors who are, in their greed, ruining all the honest sport. But the talk is most animated when out-of-the-way theories are advanced about flies. All anglers who are worthy of the name have some fancy or other about tackle. Frequently it is a "fad" rather than a well-grounded fancy, and to this all fly-fishers are very prone. The salmon-fly, being not a fly, in the sense that a March brown or Alder is an imitation of a natural insect, admits only of limited debate. There remains still, however, for settlement, the matter of gaff *versus* net, and when all else fails, old battles have to be fought over again with mighty fish, and new laments uttered over that phenomenal salmon that sulked at the bottom of the pool, and sawed away against the ledge of rock until the gut parted.

The salmon angler in action should be a strong, patient man, knowing the water he works, and the tricks and natural propensities of the game he attacks. But the process does not, in any of its stages, require such delicate manipulation as the trout angler must exercise. When you begin to handle the 18-foot rod, and run the heavy eight-plaited line through the rings, and affix the strong gut cast, with its gaudy Parson or Jock Scott, it may dawn upon the beginner, who has been accustomed to brown trout angling only, that salmon fishing, though an art, is scarcely a fine art. The downward casts, and the rough jerking movement of the fly worked through the water, do not tend to remove this impression from the mind of the angler who has been used to difficult trout fishing. The impression, in many such instances, is never wholly removed, though the capture of a few heavy fish has a wonderful effect towards creating an enthusiasm that shall abide.

But there is a majesty in a salmon river that helps to put the sportsman on terms with himself. All is movement. Born in the snow-covered mountains, the streamlet has bounded from rock to rock, whitening into cascades, broadening out into foam-flecked pools, streaming abroad over shallows and scours, gathering force down the headlong rapids, sweeping, in mature river-like dimensions, under lofty crags, eddying past dark masses of wood, and anon gently lapping yellow strands, in whose tiny wavelets children may play. Some day will come the roar of the spate, and the dark-tinted waters which call the angler to be doubly on the alert, with by-and-bye, in the dog-days, low bright streams, when his highest skill is requisite for even a small modicum of success.

February brings the opening day upon rivers such as these, with varying chances in this capricious climate— tempest to-day, north-easters, with driving sleet, and snow, and dirty water, to-morrow; but who cares if, with the fight with the elements there come at last mortal tussles with clean-run fish, though, intermingled, be the profitless hooking of foul, hungry kelts, which, be they never so well mended, must be returned to gain convalescence in the sea? Upon the banks of the Thurso, Tweed and Teviot, Tay, Lyon and Tummel; by Spey, Dee, and Don; on the turbulent surface of Loch Tay, with the shoulders of the surrounding mountains kept warm by their white mantles, the Scotch anglers ply their rods in the second month of the year, while in Ireland the lure is simultaneously cast upon the Lee and Blackwater in County Cork, the Suir above Clonmel, the Moy and lakes at Ballina, the Ballynahinch pools, the streams and lakes of County Donegal, and all kindred salmon haunts.

The trout angler who stands up for the superiority of his favourite amusement must, spite of his prejudices, admit that the capture of a salmon, upon legitimate terms, is the most exciting of all feats of piscatorial prowess. Afar off, as he fishes fruitlessly down the river bank, strewed with smooth-washed boulders, he espies the movement of a fish; not the dainty rise that scarcely attracts observation, but a heavy roll over. He has been long looking for some such token; has honestly worked every inch of the water, from the falls to the rapids, and from the rapids to this darksome pool. He has tried short casts and long casts; has humoured the fly slowly, now on the top, now sunken, and has jerked it with energy; has tried all the flies approved and recommended, small and large, and to no avail. Here at last is his chance. But nothing less than 20 yards will bring him to that unmistakable fish.

Now let him pause awhile, and run his fingers down the cast to the fly, making sure that unawares to him the tackle has not been frayed by the trial it has already undergone. Let everything be done leisurely and in order. The salmon will not move far from where the angler saw him gambolling. What he has chiefly to do is to take things quietly. He must not bother himself—I am assuming that he is not an old hand at the salmon business—by recalling all the advice he has heard and read as to the regulation conduct at this supreme moment, nor allow his attendant to disturb him with *his* advice. Let him take his own course. He has to dispatch his fly so that it shall introduce itself to salmo's notice in a genteel and natural manner. That is best accomplished by coolness; and if, coolness or not, his faculties are not at this moment all alive, and his pulses on the spring, true angler he is not.

So! The fly sped its distance, and alighted fairly well across and below, and if the angler allows the eddy from the jutting granite to take it in charge, it will be brought into position without any manœuvring on his part. Swish! It was a goodly rise, but the eager fisherman was too quick for the fish. To my thinking, that quiet intense boil in the dark current is *the* moment in salmon angling. There is a fervour in the mingling of hope, fear, and resolve that may be felt but not described, and that is not likely to recur during any of the subsequent stages of the contest. In this instance the moment of fervour would be followed by a temporary paroxysm of despair, to which the angler should not give way. He should put down his rod, seat himself on the rock, and smoke a cigarette. After all, it may have been that the salmon was too quick, and not the angler; and the fish may rise again.

The next attempt is successful, after two or three unheeded casts, but the fish rose more quietly, the fly not being so much under water, and though the rise was visible, the salmon sucked in rather than snapped at the Blue Doctor. Instead, therefore, of a boil, the fish went down with a swirling splash, and relieved the angler of half the duty of striking. Now for a brief space, to a great extent, leave the salmon to his own devices, the line never slack, the rod top well up and well curved, the winch free to respond to any demand. Nothing better could have happened than this. The fish has run at steady pace down stream. Next it may sulk or leap, requiring the angler, in the latter event, to lower his rod-point, and in the former to attach to the line the little ring which opens for the purpose, and which will run down and smite the salmon on the snout. It will be astonished and angry, but will make tracks, and so the great end is gained. Dangerous as the movement is, I rather prefer the pleasure of seeing a good fish break water, and flash his silver sides in the air, though the risk be a broken line. I would rather have a dozen somersaults than a prolonged sulk below, with that ominous trembling which so often ends in the gut being sawn off against a sharp stone. But our fish now hooked does neither. It runs up and down the pool, and continually returns to the spot where it met disaster. Finally it goes swiftly down stream, whither the angler has the opportunity of following it, and in twenty minutes the young man in attendance goes in knee deep and nets it, as it is on the point of steering once more into the stream—a fifteen-pounder, in immaculate condition.

Lucky for the angler that the finish was on that wise. Fifty yards down, the water was broken and rock-studded, and the nature of the bank fatal to any further pursuit on land. Salmon-fishing is full of such narrow escapes, and fish are not always taken with such ease. The exertion and tension of nerve undergone by the angler will nevertheless explain the possibility of a gentleman meaning what he says when he declares that, after the strike, and the first run or two, he has lost interest in the business. We have all heard of the angler who invariably hands his rod to the gillie, should the salmon play longer than ten minutes; and of the worthy who, the fish escaping after a vigorous play of forty minutes, exclaimed, "Thank God, that's over."

Salmon, however, are taken by other means than the artificial fly. Quite legitimately in Tay and other Scotch lochs, and in the Irish lakes, the fish in the spring, beginning with February, are taken with the phantom, spoon, and other artificial baits, and by spinning with the natural bait from the boat. This is, in truth, the only remunerative fashion of fishing at this period in these waters, and there is not a whisper to be breathed against the custom. But there is something unpleasant in the notion of the King of Game-fishes being done to death by a nasty blackheaded worm. Sinking and drawing with shrimp, perhaps, seems less objectionable, and when the fly is useless, as it often is in the hands of the best of anglers, conscience will tolerate minnow and par-tail rather than an empty creel. I should not like to go so far as to affirm that worm fishers for salmon and trout were poachers, but if I ever brought myself to such a pass, I would not talk about it, and should consider myself entitled to rank with the person who shoots a pheasant sitting. The end may justify the means, but it is not to be gloried in.

In February the trout angler, also welcomes his opening day. In numbers he is in the proportion of a hundred to one as compared with him of whom we have been speaking. As yet it is not the custom to impose a licence upon trout fishing, and the tickets issued by the local associations are a wholesome check upon malpractices, and no hard tax upon the fisherman. He is probably not a gentleman of leisure, or independent means, and must snatch his sport between turns at the mill-wheel of daily occupation. Very keenly, therefore, he looks forward to the opening of the rivers, and has furbished up his casts, and overhauled his rod, taken apart and oiled his winch, and arranged his flies long before the joyous day. He may have taken a preliminary Sunday ramble up the stream of his affections to make a mental map of the campaign, and be assured that the familiar scours and stickles have not been altered by the winter floods. For it will only be a dweller in the vicinity who takes earliest advantage of the February fishing—the local enthusiast who is aware that the first comer will find the trout ramping hungry in the strong currents, and so stand a good chance of sport however adverse the weather may be.

In such a climate as ours it is of course altogether too soon to talk about spring in the short, bleak, wintry February days, but for the purposes of this book we must assume that the spring begins with the 1st of February, because on many streams the close season for trout finishes on that date. At that time there are no visible signs that the winter is past, and the angler who makes up his mind to go forth must be quite independent of those sentimental thoughts which are supposed to have so large a share in the fascinations of angling. The chances are very much, however, that at the beginning of February the rivers will be unfishable. Even if frost and snow are not abroad, the streams are likely at this time of the year to be charged with flood-water, and therefore out of the question for angling.

But it is a long-established custom in Devonshire, where Nature begins to throb and move earlier than in most other parts of the country, to take advantage of the earliest fishable day after the termination of the fence months. True, the trout are seldom in condition, and ought not to be taken until March, but this is not always the case, for I myself on a frosty day on the Ottery, during a little midday sunshine, have taken at Shrovetide, which then fell in the middle of February, a brace of half-pound trout which were in as good order as any fish I have ever seen. Of course I need not remind the reader that there is no rule without an exception, and this perhaps might have been the exception. At least I made it the ground of a practical decision, acted upon in response to a dubious expression on the face of the keeper, who evidently viewed my capture of two trout from the same milky-coloured stickle with displeasure. He spoke not, but his eye most assuredly was fastened upon the second fish as he took it out of the landing-net in the hope of finding signs and tokens whereby he might invite me to return it to the water. I saw his desire, and at once pronounced the fish to be in splendid condition, a verdict with which he was bound to coincide, though he did so not very graciously, as he slipped the fish through the hole in the cover of the creel.

On the whole, therefore, though it would be impossible to pass by the month of February, we may fairly assume that it is not a valuable month for the angler, except in so far that it gives him the opportunity of getting together his tackle, and wandering out by the river side to try a few preliminary casts; and I have often been surprised to find how many anglers on the opening day of the season, let the weather be what it may, have equipped themselves, and hied them to the river, although there was not the slightest chance of getting a fish. All this, if amusing, is typical of the enthusiasm of the angler in Great Britain, and probably everywhere else. He has been waiting for this day; he has been preparing his apparatus; he has been making up his mind that now he shall have amends for the inaction of the dreary winter days. His waterproof boots are in prime order; his creel is sweet and natty; his rod has an extra polish; there is no flaw in landing-net or handle; and altogether our early angler has a very spruce appearance, when, with his heart full of hope, he goes out for the first time in the year to look for a trout. His real season, nevertheless, is more likely to begin with March.

Of Devonshire I have previously said that it still holds a first place amongst the trout-fishing counties to which the ordinary angler has access. The trout, if small, are plentiful, and there is a beauty in the county itself, and a charm in the forwardness of vegetation that make Devon very popular among anglers. The streams of Dartmoor may be taken as typical of the kind of trout stream which may be more properly termed a brook. Dartmoor, in fact, like its fishing, is a thing of itself; a wonderfully interesting solitude both for the rambler and angler. When the March brown is in its prime—although that fly may not be the best for Devonshire, where the anglers pin their faith to Meavy red, and blue upright, and hackles of various kinds—is the time to make for Dartmoor. Starting from the quiet town of Tavistock, which lies in a hollow, with the bare Cornish hills on one side and the billowy moorland on the other, you travel up-hill to Princetown, passing on the way little streams across which a strong man might easily leap, and out of which many a dish of small trout will be taken. These silvery streamlets tumble down from ledge to ledge, coming from various directions, purling through rocky little glens crowned with mystic tors, and all bound eventually to the Channel. The trout on the heights of Dartmoor are so small that the angler for awhile is ashamed to take them—ashamed until he learns how delicious the fingerlings are as served up by the Devonshire cooks, more after the fashion of whitebait, than any member of the *Salmo* family. For a man sound of wind and limb, well shod, with a small basket at his back and a light fly rod in his hand, with no necessity for carrying a landing-net, or being burdened with wading stockings or boots, a day on Dartmoor, when the wind blows well from the west on a March or April day, is a real treat, provided he be content to make it, so far as the trout are concerned, a day of small things.

March is, upon general trout streams, the first month in which fly-fishing may be hankered after in real earnest. A tempestuous, rude month it may be, but the weather is generally for the greater portion hopeful; for though the cold strengthens with the lengthening of the days, and gales prevail, there are glimpses of sunshine, and intervals of warmth which betoken the reviving year. The flies dance into life under the grateful influence, and the trout are on the look out. Later in the year you will have to ring the changes upon your stock of flies, which is generally three times as large as it need be. In March you may ordinarily rely upon the ever useful March-brown, the Blue-dun, the Olive-dun, Red Spinner, and the Marlow buzz *alias* Coch-y-bondu. Even at Lady-day the aspect of the river-side and its surroundings is bare and wintry; but when you take a short cut through the plantation to avoid the dead water, and reach the long rippling piece that murmurs down from the bridge, you will trample upon primroses and violets, and the little celandine. And the birds seem to join in a special carol of welcome to the March angler, and wish him the good fortune which often falls to his lot.

In April do not discard the above-named flies, but add to them the Grannom, Yellow-dun, Hawthorn, and Sedge, and cleave to them so long as trout-fishing lasts. April has proved to me invariably the month of months for trout in England and Wales, and would, I can fain believe, have proved so in Scotland and Ireland had I been able to subject them to the same test. If trout have feelings, they must, like the observer of nature abroad in the fields at this season, feel that it is good to be alive. They come with such a will at your flies, fight so gamely to the very end, and look so handsome in their brilliant vesture, that you linger in admiration over them in the landing-net. One or two streams in private hands are reserved for Mayday, but as a rule the British trout streams from John o'Groat's to Land's End, and from Lough Foyle to Bantry Bay, are in the prime of trout fishing in April.

Whether up-stream or down-stream fishing be the correct thing; whether gossamer casts are profitable in the long run; whether one, two or three flies should be used; whether the Alexandra fly is orthodox—these are amongst the topics the assembled fishermen discuss as they sit around on the spot to which the frugal luncheon has been brought, under shelter of the golden-blossomed gorse, their rods spiked hard by, and the flies streaming out before the breeze. If there are more than two present there is not likely to be unanimity upon any of these points.

It is well for the tackle makers that new notions—heresies in the eyes of anglers of the last generation—are so freely promulgated. I know some successful fishermen who habitually fish down-stream, and who use medium gut for their casts. In very rapid water, free from weeds (the Derbyshire rivers, and Welsh streams, for example,) a third fly may be added to the stretcher and dropper, but, on the whole, little good comes of more than two flies on the cast. In trout water where the fish do not rise well at the usual flies the Alexandra is as much in place as a spun minnow, but it spoils the fish for the artificial fly pure and simple. Upon all these matters the angler must form his own judgments from experience, and then I fancy he will take a delight, when wading, in casting straight up-stream with a short line; will always, otherwise, aim at casting across and allowing the flies to drift down without worrying them as they swim; and when a quick current, or impediments ashore leave no alternative, will do the best within his power, down-stream, underhand, or by that curious pitch which the angler learns to make with effect when he has an obstacle at his back. When he has achieved the art of throwing a fly without frightening away the fish he has conquered the primary difficulty.

April brings an opening day for the Thames trout-fisher. The Thames trout, by careful preservation and the introduction of new stock, have not for many years given so good an account of themselves as during the season of 1883, and even after its close on the 15th September, a provokingly large quantity took a fancy to the baits of barbel-fishers, who returned them, as in duty bound, to the river. Trouting on the Thames is, however, indulged in by the few rather than the many. Only the most patient men follow it through evil and good report. It makes an abnormal draft upon human faith; it is a somewhat sedentary occupation, as followed by modern masters. Now and then this notable fish is taken with an artificial fly, but fly-fishing is seldom practised by the regular Thames trout angler. You will find this worthy mostly perched above the head of one of the weirs, of which Boveney is a more than average sample, spinning a bleak in the streams and rough water under his feet, not, however, if he understand his business, leaving the bait to work its own restless will, and fruitlessly revolve on the top of the foam, but cleverly humouring it right and left, in eddies, down the current, and so making it dart and move that its action is calculated to deceive the very elect amongst Thames trout, the most knowing perhaps of any of the *Fario* family.

Spinning for Thames trout, whether from weir or boat,

is work for none but accomplished artists, and there are upon the river a few renowned specialists who day by day, and week by week, pursue their sport with untiring devotion, though a fish or two per week throughout the season would be considered very excellent sport. The Thames trout, however, is a gallant battler when once he feels the little triangles in his palate. While the rush lasts he outdoes even the salmon in his fierce charges and desperate tactics, so that, if he be discovered but rarely, when he does make a grave error he is a foeman worthy of the best steel ever fashioned into a fish-hook.

The game goes on until the 15th September, but the bloom is taken off the sport in a couple of months from the opening day. Every weir is spun persistently, and every weir, perhaps, if it could reveal its secrets, would testify to fish that had broken away, been pricked, or otherwise put upon their guard. Thus the trout, already cunning, get exceedingly wary, and hard to catch. Once upon a time the Thames anglers never dreamt of looking for trout in other than weirpools and rough, swift water, but modern men have found out that in reaches of the river where their presence was never suspected, an occasional lusty patriarch, retired from the noise and perpetual motion of lasher and weir, has taken up a quiet haunt; and as, in his more lively foraging expeditions, he is certain, sooner or later, to let his whereabouts be known—since the Thames is not hid in a corner—the process of live-baiting is applied to him, and not infrequently with fatal results.

CHAPTER III.

SUMMER.

SUMMER angling brings out new and more miscellaneous forces than heretofore to promote designs upon our fresh-water fishes, and the English ladies are taking very kindly both to fly-fishing and general fishing. May they never be persuaded into pleading their sex as an excuse for establishing unsportsmanlike practices against salmon and trout? Fly rods are made so daintily now, and casting a fly is really so easy, when once the knack is acquired of permitting the rod to do the major part of the work, that want of strength is no plea. And there is a still better argument. Not even the harp or the violin, nor the lawn-tennis racket, shows off the female figure to such positive advantage as the graceful manipulation of the fly-rod. In the summer evenings, therefore, when there is a saunter through the hay-field to the river and its forget-me-nots, listen not to the assurances of the youth (who knows better) that when ladies fish for the speckled beauties of the stream any bait may be used. He may be deprived of that coveted chance of impaling the worms for the fair fisherwoman, but his conscience will be at peace if he recommend and teach her the use of the fly.

The Mundella Act sets loose the fishing-punts on the 15th of June, when we may reasonably assume that summer smiles upon the land. On Thames, and such inland waters as come under the operations of the measure, the anglers swarm to renew their acquaintance with roach, dace, barbel, chub, perch, and (sad to add) with pike. Throughout the summer angling is made the occasion of happy water picnics. Hot bright days will mostly find all but the surface-feeding fish ensconced within the cool shady arbours of their subaqueous abodes, and morning and evening are the anglers' likeliest times for sport. The carp, however,—rarest of objects in the fisherman's basket—loves the blazing summer weather, and on intervening cloudy days may be hooked unawares. The long days are welcome to the angler on account of the spells of calm evening fishing afforded; and a traveller rushing through the kingdom by any of the main lines of railway will be able to observe how universally popular is the amusement. By river, lake, canal, pond, clay-pit, and ditch, coming within ken of his carriage window, he will behold its persevering followers.

In the pond out of which the horses come to slake their thirst after the day's team-work is over, the schoolboy, having got through, at scampering pace, to-morrow's lessons, is allowed to make his first essays in angling; and perhaps to the majority of us those juvenile snatches of fishing, with tackle of the most primitive kind, live longest in the memory, not only because of the singular passion for the sport which takes root in the boyish mind never to be eradicated, but because of the wonderful luck which proverbially falls to the neophyte's share. How often does it happen that the expert fisherman, with his delicate silk line and drawn gut links, with his carefully chosen baits, and working with all the wisdom of mature experience, has the mortification of seeing some untutored rustic walking away with a string of fish, while his basket remains untenanted! And in some of those out-of-the-way ponds in rural England—ponds that have held fish from time immemorial—there is rare sport to be obtained on summer evenings with the mud-loving tench and the undaunted perch, descendants, may be, of the same fish which the Puritan lads caught in the days before their father's farm was drenched with the blood of Cavalier and Roundhead. On warm muggy days when all creation seems to sweat, and there is thunder in the air, that singular fish, the tench, bites well, and the largest and most plentiful of them are to be found in the most ancient of park lakes and monastic ponds. The sport is not particularly exciting, but it requires to be conducted with great care on account of the shyness of the fish. Different is it with the pond perch, which is a great encouragement to the youthful angler by the reckless readiness with which it will, in its hungry moments, assist him in imbibing a lifelong taste for the pastime.

In the vicinity of large towns the angler sits by the water side breathing at least fresh air, and surrounded by sights calculated to make him forget the petty cares of life, or the sordid belongings of a lot of poverty. He is content with even the smallest result in the way of sport. That sport is not of an extensive kind, nor of a high class, but he enjoys it, and appreciates his little show of roach or dace, or barbel, as much as the man of means appreciates his trout or salmon.

Summer time is also the period when that very remarkable collection of fresh-water lakes known as the broads of East Anglia are laid under contribution by anglers and cruisers. These broads have a character of their own in the angling of Great Britain, teeming as they do with bream and other coarse fish. It is no uncommon thing in a cruise up the waters from Lowestoft and Yarmouth, or from Wroxham Bridge, which is the starting-point for the upper broads, to pass hundreds of boats, each filled with its earnest angling party.

There are in these waters roach and perch and pike, bream and rudd, in untold quantities, but the reed thickets surrounding them are so dense that the pike are not generally enticed out of them until the winter, when the other kinds have retired to the deeps. The bream are so numerous that they are reckoned by the stone rather than by the brace or dozen, and although they are not highly-esteemed for table purposes after they are caught, they furnish a good deal of fun in the catching. This operation is somewhat disagreeable to a fastidious person. The angler provides himself with a huge bucket containing a sloppy mixture of grains and meal, and he protects himself from stray *débris* by wearing a white apron. This compound is thrown broadcast into a particular pitch—it should be done overnight—and the bream collect in herds around it. The hook is baited with a worm or with gentles, and the fish, when they are fairly on the feed, bite without cessation until the store net, which the East Anglian angler keeps suspended over the side of the punt, is full of large broad-sided, bronze-coloured bream, averaging 3 or 4 lbs.

These broads are also a favourite hunting-ground of the rudd, a fish often confounded with the roach. It is confined to a comparatively few localities, and there is no mistaking its lovely golden jacket and carmine fins and irides. Though commonly angled for on the same principle as roach, it will rise very freely at a fly in hot weather. In the quiet evenings, after the sun is down, I have moored my rude boat to the reeds that border one of these meres, and whipped out two half-pound rudd at a time, as fast as I could introduce to the shoal my small black gnat or red palmer, with a gentle on the tip of the hook. You could see the whole shoal rising at the small insects that were humming in the summer air.

Here a man is out of the noise and turmoil of the world. For leagues the eye roams over the tranquil waters, or upon the flat peculiar country converted by the slow running rivers, abundant windmills, and far-reaching broads, into a very Dutch-like kind of scenery. Nothing breaks the silence but the plunge of big fish amongst the reeds, or the constant passage of water-fowl, for which the region is as celebrated as for its coarse fish. When the gentlemen of Norfolk kindly invited the foreign commissioners at the International Fisheries Exhibition to go and inspect this region, Mr. Wilmot of the Canadian Court, and Professor Brown Goode of the United States Commission, expressed an opinion that the waters were very suitable for the introduction of the black bass. This fish has already been acclimatised by the Marquis of Exeter, and from its game qualities, its freedom in rising at a fly, or taking a spinning bait, it would be a very welcome addition to our fresh-water fishes, and would take an intermediate position between the pike and the perch, and the members of the Salmonidæ family. And it would be easy to confine the black bass to waters where it would not destroy more valuable species. Whether the gentlemen who have formed themselves into a society to protect the fisheries of these broads will entertain such an idea, or whether they will act upon a more recent suggestion and attempt the introduction of salmon, remains to be seen. The broads, at any rate, cannot be omitted from a description of our angling waters; they are visited every summer by thousands of anglers from various parts of the country, and are well worth visiting.

According to the terms of the Mundella Act, as I have stated, the Thames fisherman has his opening day on the 15th June, although it is much too soon to angle for pike. The other fish, if not in fair condition, are rapidly arriving at that stage, and from this date the professional fisherman hopes to have his regular customers, and each favourite station of the Thames will have its periodical visits from anglers. The efforts of the Thames Angling P'reservation Society have undoubtedly been crowned with success, for the stock of fish has been improving year by year, and, as a passing reference in the previous chapter shows, the angling of the present season has been in all parts satisfactory. The Thames anglers are somewhat of a school to themselves, and, moreover, a very numerous class. They have a variety of fishing at their disposal. Roach and dace are plentiful everywhere from Kew to the source. Barbel are taken at certain stations in bulk. Pike too and perch are equally distributed along the whole length of the beautiful river, and the **fly-fisher** has plenty of room for the exercise of his abilities with chub and dace.

Fly-fishing for chub answers best in the hot summer months—say July and August; and along the willow and alder lined reaches, at odd times payable sport is obtained. It is a great boon after all for the man in the big city pent to be able to get away from business, and by an afternoon train arrive at any portion of the Thames below Oxford in time to have three or four of the best hours' **fly-fishing** which the day affords. The chub is not fastidious in its choice of flies. So long as the lure is large and hairy; so long as it bears some passing resemblance to a caterpillar or beetle, or large-winged moth, the angler's chances of big fish are good. The chub, however, is an easily scared fish, and it is a primary essential that the whipper shall keep out of sight.

The breadth of such rivers as the Thames at Moulsford,

or Ouse below St. Ives, and the out-of-the-way places in which the chub loves to lie, render the use of a boat imperative. In this the angler stations himself in the stern, his boatmen allowing the craft to drift slowly with the stream ten or twelve yards abreast of the overhanging branches, under which he knows the fish are lying. Let the fly touch the leaves, and then make believe to tumble accidentally into the water. There will be a straight rush made by the chub (which is not at all insulted in the old-fashioned appellation of logger-headed); he will take your fly at a gulp under water without the ceremony of a rise; and the leathery formation of the mouth makes the chances of escape very poor for the fish. The chub has no character for pluck, since after one pretty strong run by way of protest, it ceases to fight, and may be hauled into the landing-net without much trouble or the employment of any art on the part of the angler. I have known gentlemen in the course of a few hours' fishing in this manner take their 20 and 30 lbs. of chub, ranging from 2 to 4 lbs. In the Upper Verniew in the month of April three years ago, at one stand, fishing for trout with a small March brown, I took 18 chub of about a pound each. If they had weighed not more than a pennyweight I would have killed them in any trout water.

Trout-fishing I have dealt with in one or two phases in the chapter on spring. It need scarcely, however, be explained that this fish is the fly-fisher's idol during the entire summer. But the carnival of trout anglers may be said to occur when the May-fly is up. This anxiously looked for event generally happens early in June, and while it lasts the sport is indeed fast and furious. On preserved club waters, like the Hungerford water of the Kennet, and on the choice preserves of Hampshire, and other parts of the West of England, the sportsmen turn out with one consent to take advantage of the seven devils of gluttony which seem to enter into the strong-minded trout.

It is a glorious time of the year in which to be abroad on such a quest. The honey-suckle is opening its buds in the leafy lanes, the satin blossoms of the bramble are put forth, the rich meadows are ready for the haymakers, the foliage of the woods is developed upon nearly all our English trees, the wild flowers are spangling field and hedgerow in their glory, and the cuckoo, making the most of the little time that is left for song, "Tells his name to all the hills."

But I should say that at no season of the year has the sentimental angler less time than now to indulge in rhapsodies, for when the green and grey drake are what is technically termed "up," sport will demand all his attention. Lucky he if it make him not a butcher. There was a deal of human nature in that eminent divine who, upon being asked by his friend the bishop when an important work upon which he was engaged would be finished, replied—" My lord, I shall work steadily at it when the fly-fishing season is over." Such a reference, we may be permitted to believe, could only have been prompted by an unusually exuberant "great rise" in the May-fly season.

And no one has in pithier words described the peculiarities of this festival than Charles Kingsley, who, in his 'Chalk Stream Studies,' says:—"For is not the green drake on? And while he reigns, all hours, meals, decencies, and respectabilities must yield to his caprice. See here he sits, or rather tens of thousands of him, one on each stalk of grass, green drake, yellow drake, brown drake, white drake, each with his gauzy wings folded over his back, waiting for some unknown change of temperature or something else, in the afternoon, to wake him from his sleep, and send him fluttering over the stream; while overhead the black drake, who has changed his skin and reproduced his species, dances in the sunshine, empty, hard, and happy, like Festus Bailey's great black crow, who

> 'All his life sings ho! ho! ho!
> For no one will eat him he well doth know.'"

The peculiarities of May-fly fishing are so well known, that there would be no excuse for pausing longer upon the subject. Bungling indeed must be the angler who cannot during this space of ten or twelve days catch fish, and the barefacedness with which, under favourable circumstances, the trick is done, rather leads one to regret that on any English stream the custom still prevails of fishing for trout with a living instead of artificial May-fly. The angler who cannot score with one of the perfect imitations now turned out, ought not to have a second chance.

It is different in the celebrated lakes of West Meath, where the big fish are not readily taken by the artificial fly, and where it has been an immemorial custom to use the impaled live insect with the blow line. Upon these lakes, for which Mullingar, some forty miles from Dublin, might be made convenient headquarters, the green drake comes up in myriads. The brown trout which the waters contain are in takeable condition as early as March, and are to be enticed with some of the common artificial flies used in the spring months. The most knowing fishermen in the drake season use two hooks tied back to back, and two flies so arranged that the head of one shall lie next to the tail of the other. The surface of the lakes, amongst which I may mention Ennel, or Belvidere, Owel, and Lough Ree (through which the Shannon runs), is agitated all over with the rising of fish that are seldom less than two pounds, and that run even to the maximum size of six and seven pounds. The boat is rowed up against the wind, and allowed to drift back broadside on.

The angler uplifts his moderately stiff rod, to which is attached the line of floss silk, very flimsy in appearance, but in reality strong enough for all necessary purposes. This the wind takes out, and the art is to allow the flies to dance upon the surface of the water as if a fancy-free insect were sailing along, tacking here and there with outspread wings, as is its pretty custom. It, however, requires a little experience to get into the way of striking the fish with a line which is naturally considerably bellied out at the time the bait is taken; but practice here, as in other things, soon makes perfect, and astonishing bags of trout are made.

This blow line fishing might in the summer be used with advantage to a greater extent than it is at present in English waters. In the Lea I have seen masterful baskets of roach, chub, and dace, acquired by this device; the hook attached to the blow-line in such cases, however, being very small, and the insect a house fly, or some other creature of no more formidable size and character. Roach will occasionally, I may mention in passing, take the artificial fly, especially when to it is appended the luscious gentle; but this only happens in the very hottest weather, when the fish are lazy on the shallows. But the blow-line invariably agitates, and often catches them.

On the disappearance of the May fly the trout become demoralized. They have gorged to their heart's content, and probably a little more, for their voracity during the term (it is commemoration term with the angler) in which the fly is up is such that you often take the fish crammed with them, and with a little bunch of flies waiting at the threshold of the gullet for a favourable opportunity of being absorbed into the stomach. I have seen a May-fly crawl out of the half-opened mouth of a trout in my basket.

It is not to be wondered at that after this debauchery a certain supineness intervenes, and that the trout lie about in a depressed state of mind, such as should always follow immoderation of appetite. Upon some rivers, indeed, the pick of the trout fishing is over after the May-fly time, while in others, as in the Gloucestershire Coln, the really best fishing does not begin until the trout have recovered from their periodical feast. As the summer advances the trout fisher enters into another phase of his artistic sport, perhaps the most delicate of all. The rivers run low, the weeds form thickets and forests in the streams. The trout, much whipped over during the preceding three or four months, have become disagreeably artful, and if they are to be caught at all they must be caught by guile.

Guile in this particular instance takes the shape of what is termed fishing with a dry fly. Of late years the tackle-makers have arrived at the perfection of art in manufacturing what should be to the fish the most ravishing of artificial flies, whose upstanding wings materially assist the angler in this very artful angling operation. At the same time, I ask permission to believe that trout fishermen are apt to ride the dry fly notion to death. When once some of us get into the habit of using the dry fly, and wax proud of our ability, we become wedded to the method, and in season and out of season adhere to it. At times it is unquestionably absolutely necessary to use the dry fly, for the best of all reasons—the fish will look at no other. But I have frequently seen experienced anglers persevere with their floating fancies, yet do nothing, when other persons who were allowing their flies to sink and swim in the usual way down the stream were rewarded with trout.

It is always useful, nevertheless, to have your supply of dry flies at hand, and in case of non-success in the other method, to put them up. But, I repeat, too much is oftentimes made of the dry-fly theory. Perhaps this is because of a consciousness on the part of the angler that it requires the acme of skill to be successful with it. Perhaps, also, it may be partly accounted for by the said angler being used to waters where dry-fly fishing in the later months of the summer is a *sine quâ non*.

There are no more skilful trout anglers than those accustomed to the streams which flow tranquilly through the fat Hampshire meadows. The rivers contain beautiful fish, but they are extremely difficult to take, and the Hampshireman is quite justified in his boast that the angler who can kill in Itchen or Test need not be ashamed to exhibit his prowess anywhere. It requires a good deal of experience to learn how, after whipping the fly four or five times through the air, to secure the requisite dryness, to dispatch it across underneath the further bank, and make it alight so that it shall float some distance down the stream without being checked by the line.

The situation necessarily involves a certain slackness of line, and with the fine tackle that must be used, the extra skill, of which I have just spoken, must be extended to the striking, else a long farewell to fly and fish. There is no doubt that a large percentage of trout hooked in dry-fly fishing by defect at this crisis get away. I know of no more pleasant form of angling for trout on a fine summer's evening, when a mere zephyr skims over the water, when the swallows are hawking low upon it, and the voice of the corncrake is heard in the uplands, than to kneel warily amongst the flowering comfrey, meadow sweet, willow herb, and loosestrife, and mark a rising trout close under the rank sedges fringing yonder bank. The artificial sedge fly, with its artistic ribbing, though not made expressly to float, is capital for dry-fly fishing, and all things being favourable there is no more telling way of adding to the contents of your basket than by finishing up a day's fishing in laying siege to that fish till he capitulates.

Then in August the red and black ant come in, and all through the summer three specific flies should never be out of the angler's book, to wit the Wickham, Hoflands, and the Francis Francis Fancies. During the past season I was introduced by my friend Mr. Marston to a new fly, new at least to me, the wings of which are made of pike scales. It is manufactured by McNee of Pitlochrie, and I have found it answer, and seen it answer, when the trout allowed every other kind of fly to pass by unheeded. The theory is that the pike scale, when it becomes wet, has the unctuous appearance of a gelatinous wing, and it may be so. At any rate, on streams as opposite in their character as the Chatsworth Derwent, the Little Stour in Kent, and the Lambourne in Berkshire, I have reason to be thankful that this addition to our list of flies was made known to me. It is certainly worth a trial.

Loch fishing is a fashionable and essential item of the general summer programme, and on Loch Leven the club competitions for which the lake is celebrated are decided. It is truly astonishing that the trout in this lake show no signs of diminution, for although careful restocking is attended to, there is no more thoroughly thrashed water in Scotland; and amongst the gentlemen who make such pleasant parties in the boats 'you generally find one who has never handled rod before, and whose flies do *not* fall like the traditional thistledown upon the water. Yet the sport, if not what it was when an angler was disgusted if he came ashore at Kinross without his twenty or thirty pounds of fish, is maintained above an ordinary level. In the year before last, I can recall one day in May, when seventeen boats were on the lake—a full complement. The wind and water were favourable, and the boats finished in the evening with 212 trout, weighing 213 lbs. The Loch Leven trout always seem to average one pound; and as I have watched anglers from Edinburgh, Dundee, Glasgow, Stirling, Perth, Kirkcaldy, and Dunfermline, I have often thought that their tackle is unnecessarily coarse. No doubt they know their own business best. They get fine sport certainly.

Different from Leven are the lochs away in the unbeaten districts of the Highlands. There is the small lake swarming with yellow trout of three to the pound (game little fellows to angle for on a summer day), and there is the larger loch in which the pike keep down the small fish, so that the angler will get none under two pounds. The brown trout attain a heavy size—five, six, and seven pounds—in these waters, and, unlike the *ferox*, they will take a large fly with gusto. Spinning with a phantom minnow of medium size, when the natural bait cannot be procured, is useful for all these large trout, and for salmon. In the streams the summer warrants the use of Stewart's tackle, a most telling method, which one may almost describe as fly-fishing with worm. I have seen it applied by southerners in southern waters with surprising results in perch and chub fishing.

CHAPTER IV.

AUTUMN.

THERE is a charm in the English autumn to which the angler ought to be peculiarly sensible. The late coming salmon and sea-trout fishing, wind and weather permitting, is the best of the year, since it is not, in the natural order of things, interfered with by the turbulent floods which follow the melting of the snow, nor reduced by the netters, nor ruined by the low, bright waters of the summer weeks. Autumn is more often reliable, I have noticed, as to weather than other seasons, though there was a miserable exception to the rule in 1882. When the elements are favourable, the water is in excellent condition for the Scotch, Irish, English and Welsh streams visited by the migratory salmon.

The days, which rapidly close in long before the swallows depart or the leaves fall, are all too short, however, for such out-of-door sports as angling, because the fish have now no inclination to move freely until the forenoon is well advanced. Against this drawback must be written the exquisite tints of the trees, and the bracing air, in which the more active exercises of angling may be conducted in comfort. For spinning or trolling, for wielding the big greenheart, the double-handed hickory, or the split cane single-hander, there are no better months than September and October; and as to landscape, I am one of those who love spring, revel in summer, but adore autumn, with its corn and wine and oil, its golden plenty emphasised by a framework of gentle decay.

The salmon fisher has seen the brown hills brighten with green, and blaze into the regal purple of the heather, and now the rowan tree hangs out its scarlet lamps, and the firs assume a deeper hue. The trout fisher in the bright May days was gladdened by the fragrant hawthorn, and noticed how strong the briony clasped the hedgerow. He saw the blossoms of the wild guelder rose shaken to earth by the lightest summer shower, and the true wild rose in full bearing. Their berries now gleam black and red, those of the guelder rose clustered like drops of blood, while its leaves are veined with every colour of the rainbow. The village children, who months back stood shyly by to watch the landing of the two-pounder that had taken the Red Spinner in the smooth stream above the ford, had sprigs of immature travellers' joy round their hats, and their hands were full of cowslip, ragged robbin, and lady smocks. Their faces are smeared with blackberry stain, and their pinafores turned into receptacles for hazel nuts, as they wonder why, on that late September evening, you cast your fly so many times through the air before allowing it to touch the water. The punt fisher moored in the Thames above Maidenhead, has, in Bisham, and incomparable Cliveden, a mixture of colours upon the densely wooded hillsides such as mortal hand could never compound.

The sea-trout fisher is in his glory in the autumn. That last run up of the fish is generally the briskest, and the sea-trout angler has therefore the privilege of leaving off for the season without the consciousness that it was convenient to make a virtue of necessity. So long as the *Salmo Irutta* is in the river, you do not wear out your welcome. This fish gives super-excellent sport. Your equipment is heavier than that used for brown trout, and lighter than salmon gear. A well-balanced double-handed rod that will answer also for grils is the weapon, and there is no need whatever for the coarse gut footline which in both Scotland and Ireland the native anglers deem essential. The gut must be of the purest quality, but medium size is ample. The difficulty here is to obtain flies that are tied upon gut to correspond, and this is a difficulty which causes annoyance to all classes of anglers. It is a forcible argument in favour of the new fashion of eyed flies for every description of fly fishing. The sea-trout is found in most salmon rivers, of course, and in the lakes, but his chief recommendation to me is that he runs up small streams, which but for him would never be visited by any of the silvery visitors.

There is in my mind's eye at the present a narrow river, if I may so term it, which has no name upon the map. Within a hundred yards of the sea I could leap across it in two places. You can reach its infant stage by tramping a couple of miles up the moor through a heathery bog, and follow it down through, at first, a series of rough, rocky leaps, next through a sequestered glen, and finally through a descending mile of turning and twisting. This streamlet, up to the heaped-up rocklets, is a succession of pools and streams, alternating with perfectly dull water. In the autumn the sea-trout swarm in every one of them, though they do not reach the maximum size. In the next river on the same coast, and not twenty miles distant, five-pound fish are not rare, but in my nameless stream you create a sensation at the village post-office—which is the Rialto of that Highland community—if you kill one of three pounds. Two pounds seems to be an average, and may I never meet with worse sport than a couple of dozen sea-trout in such condition and of such dimensions, fairly caught with the fly.

The sea-trout fights in a manner of his own. His first dashes are as fierce as those of the Thames trout, but (for his size) he keeps the game up longer, and has some special gift at leaping out of the water. It was not until I had caught a few sea-trout that I comprehended how it could be possible for a man, who had the instincts of a true sportsman, to treat with contempt all fresh-water fish but sea-going Salmonidæ. Numbers of Scotch anglers deem even brown trout unworthy of notice, and they are generally men who have been fortunate enough to be able to fish for sea-trout, and on privileged occasions a salmon, in their younger days. The sea-trout soon steals into your affections. He is so elegant in shape, so full of health and life, so active in his movements, so plucky in resisting the doom to which the angler (who loves him so much) consigns him—a justifiable doom, nevertheless, for the sea-trout is a fish that will not disgrace any table.

The Welsh sewin is nothing like so reliable as a sport-yielder as the *trutta*, if, indeed, what you are assured is a sewin should happen to be the bull-trout, as in the majority of instances it will prove to be. He is not a ravenous riser at the fly, though in this respect he is more charitable in his actions than the great lake trout of Ireland and Scotland. The Coquet is the British stream most frequented by *Salmo eriox*, and the lusty fish run to ten or twelve pounds, and sometimes to sixteen or eighteen pounds. You rarely bag them so large in the south Welsh streams, and in fly-fishing two and three pound fish are as much as you can expect. More than half of the fish called sewin by Welsh anglers are *Salmo trutta*, to whose healthy appetites flies never come amiss. But the smaller bull-trout come sometimes liberally to the fly-fisher of Wales, whose best flies are our old friend the March brown, locally known as the Cob, the Bittern, and the Coch-y-bondu, all tied large. You cast down and work your lines as with sea-trout and salmon.

The ancient legend by which we are assured that our forefathers believed that the grayling was introduced into this country by the monks, seems by modern authorities to be somewhat discredited. Let us hope this scepticism does not arise from a mean spirit of sectarian animosity, from a desire, in point of fact, to rob the reverend fathers of the credit that attaches to a work so undoubtedly meritorious.

Whether the fish be indigenous or not, after all, matters very little. We may be thankful that they abound. They are such a blessing to the angler, that I believe there would be little difficulty in raising a marble monument to the man who could be proved to have introduced the grayling into English waters, for the fish is, in truth, entitled to most affectionate regard. When trout-fishing is done with, grayling-fishing is within a month of its zenith, and right away through December, January, and February, in the middle hours of the day, when the sun shines, though the ground be hard with frost, and the snow glistens upon branch and bank (so long as there is no snow broth in the water), the grayling will rise steadily at the fly. The streams of Herefordshire I have already referred to as great in stores of grayling, and the Hampshire waters are almost as good; in the opinion, perhaps, of the Hampshire fishermen themselves, better. Yorkshire, again, has plenty of grayling streams, the chief of which is the Wharfe. Although the fishing within a mile either way of Bolton Abbey is scarcely worth a trial now, below the Duke's waters, and, again, a few miles above Bolton Abbey, the sport is good.

We will, for a moment, take the Bolton Abbey water as a general type of the river in which grayling will thrive. Towards the end of October the yellow and brown leaves are beginning to scatter before the blast, and their presence in the stream is sometimes almost as much a nuisance to the angler as the disgusting little midgelet, not inaptly called "the angler's curse," is in summer time to the trout fisher. The fall of the leaf and activity amongst grayling men are synonymous. At the wider end of our limit, we begin with a long stretch of shallow water rippling at the uniform depth of a foot over amber-coloured pebbles and gravels. Here you would naturally expect to take trout in the early part of the year; but you would waste your time in whipping for grayling. Wait until you pass through into the next field; there you will find that the river takes a sudden swerve to the right, flowing deep at the bottom of the woods opposite, and washing up at your feet, as you stand by the brink on your own side, from a shelf which gradually slopes to the deepest part. At the upper end of the curve, there is something in the nature of a fall, caused by large blocks of boulder, and in the very eye of the sharp stream formed by them, you may make certain of a rise. Also in the smooth gliding water, five or six feet deep, though it may be in the bend of the curve, you should, with red tag, or a tiny floating dun, or one of those queer little spiders in fashion in the district, pick out your pound grayling; while at the tail of the stream where it escapes in an oily fashion from the depth of the pool is another favourite haunt.

In Dovedale, again, is a noted grayling water, to which disciples of Walton and Cotton devote loyal pilgrimages.

The Derbyshire streams I must needs once more mention, for it is a boon indeed to the English angler at large, that proprietors, like the Duke of Devonshire, allow the public, under reasonable regulations, to fish them. One of the cross-purposes so often experienced by the angler arises from these rivers, which contain both trout and grayling. How frequently it occurs in all grayling streams, that while you are fishing for trout in the summer, you hook grayling, whereas when the trout are black and foul, and you are trying diligently for grayling, the unseasonable fish will make gratuitous onslaughts upon your fly!

The grayling is not given to leaping out of the water, but he makes amends whenever you bring him to the surface, by floundering about in a position more dangerous in a tender-mouthed fish than leaping; so that unless you are careful, the grayling, by the free exercise of that large and beautifully tinted dorsal-fin, will contrive to escape at the very moment when you have made sure of him. There are waters in which you may fish for trout with medium-sized casts, but this will not do for grayling. The very finest tackle is required for them. As, however, they often lie deep, and make nothing of darting straight upwards three or four feet to take the fly that is floating down above them, the grayling fisher is not required to crouch upon all-fours, or kneel by the river side as in summer-trouting.

There is a dispute, which is not of much importance, amongst some grayling-anglers, as to what this dainty fish smells like. Some swear by thyme, from which the fish receives the name of *Salmo thymallus*, whilst others have a notion that cucumber would be nearer the mark; and there is a fish in Australasia which is as often called the cucumber fish as the Australian grayling.

An English grayling of about 1½ lbs. weight is as handsome in his own peculiar style of beauty as the trout, for if he lack the crimson spots and golden burnishment, he has a fine admixture of blue and silver, while his shape is faultless.

There is another kind of fly-fishing to be followed during September and October, of which I for one am extremely fond, albeit it has a somewhat unpretentious object, being directed to nothing more important than the common dace. The dace is really one of our surface feeders. He may be found during the winter time in deep water, keeping company with the roach, and he congregates in force in deep mill-tails and weir-pools, where he will take the small red worm or the gentle with very much the boldness of the perch. In Autumn, however, the dace still lingers upon the shallows, and rises well at almost any small fly. Take two examples of dace-fishing in the autumn. The first was in the Thames, above Richmond Bridge. All the shallows, from Twickenham downwards, have a well deserved repute for fly-fishing for dace, and the Thames-side urchins, with willow-wands, lengths of whipcord, and anything in the shape of a fly which they can beg or borrow, make nice little strings of fish, running to about seven or eight inches in length. A sunshiny day, with a soft ripple, is the best for this sport, and one might pass away four or five hours in worse amusement than wading into the Thames opposite Ham Lane, and whipping down upon the shallows with the fancy black and red flies manufactured for the purpose, their speciality being tiny strips of wash-leather, in place of tail. There is a continual procession of pleasure-boats up this gay reach of the Thames, and the familiar features of Richmond Hill are an elevated background to the picture which the downward moving angler looks upon. It is useless fishing for dace in the Thames, except at particular times of the tide, and the regular plan is to begin when the tide is at half-ebb, and leave off when the flood makes. A working-man angler, who was standing a few yards above me, on the last occasion I indulged in this amusement, whipped out, with very indifferent tackle, his four dozen of fish, and I myself, had something over three dozen of the silvery little fellows in my basket.

A seven-inch, however, or even a nine-inch dace (and you will seldom get larger specimens while fly-fishing on the Thames shallows) is very indifferent game as compared with the really good-looking and gamesome fish of the same species which are to be had in the Colne and in the Lea. On the second occasion to which I have referred, I was taken by a gentleman to a choice club water on the Lea, between Hertford and Ware. A mill pool was pointed out to me as full of dace. The mill was silent, and there was no stream from the pool; but a light breeze tickled its surface, and the sun was shining in a cloudless sky. The sides of the mill pool were solid masonry, and the pool terminated in a somewhat sudden shelf. The stream thenceforward, for some hundred yards, was of the shallowest description. One does not often get the opportunity of fly-fishing from a seat, but I was in an indolent humour on this particular morning, and sat me down on the edge of the wall, with my feet dangling over the stream, some 10 yards below the tail of the pool. The fish, for an hour or so, were perfectly ravenous, and gave me much entertainment. There were very few dace under $\frac{1}{2}$ lb., and fat lively white fellows of that kind upon a drawn-gut cast, and with the smallest trout-rod that is made, will treat you to no indifferent sport. Within

F

a short space of time I contrived to get from the pool, or from the two-inch shallows down stream, nine and a half brace of specimen dace, which, with the addition of a few others contributed by my friend, made the total weight nearly 10 lbs.

We have glanced at the grand salmon rivers and the swift trout streams, and at the more sluggish rivers by which the general angler watches his travelling float, or keeps the tightened leger line well in hand. Lakes and ponds, amidst the "tall ancestral trees" of country domains, have not been forgotten. But autumn reminds me of yet another haunt of the English angler. It is the millpool, within the upper wall of which the waterwheel drippingly revolves, grinding the corn of the miller and his men. Not less dear to the angler than the poet and artist is the English mill. Above the mill head there is often a quiet reach, permanently tenanted by pike and perch.

From the pool miscellaneous bags are extracted. The live bait works on its own accord on the other side under the graceful willows, while the angler, with his ordinary rod, line, and float, angles promiscuously. Out of such a millpool I have seen, lying in one heap upon the grass behind some old woodwork upon which the angler sat, a representative sample of many British fresh-water fishes, and as they were caught on an October day, they were all, with one exception, in their healthiest hues and forms. The heap comprised a 7 lb. pike, four or five burly perch, a brown and a white bream, several roach and dace, one gudgeon, four minnows, and a small barbel. The exception indicated was an indiscreet trout, which had taken a gudgeon on the live-bait apparatus, and since the hook used was the gorge affair that is threddled under the skin of the side, the case was hopeless, and the kindly miller, on being appealed to, decided that the fish should not be returned to die a painful death.

The autumnal general-fishing of the rivers produces, as a rule, larger fish than are taken in the summer. The weeds soon begin to rot after Michaelmas, and most of the coarse fish betake themselves, without more ado, to their winter quarters in the deeps. The prettiest hour's roach fishing I ever saw was on a September evening, on returning from whipping a ford where the large dace were in the habit of congregating. Above one of those small noisy weirs which are laid across our lesser rivers, there meandered through the meadow some 200 yards of even current, still but deep. There were three rustic seats stationed upon the bank, for the convenience of the members of the club who rented the fishery. Upon one of these sat a veteran angler, who had had his share of the more energetic descriptions of sport for half a century, and who was now content with the tranquil amusement of roach fishing. He thoroughly understood the art, and would have deemed that the roach were insulted if angled for with other than a tight hair line and a long bamboo rod. His process was troublesome, but remunerative. At every swim he enveloped his paste bait with a thin wrapping of the bran composition with which he had been ground-baiting, and it was a liberal education to watch his fortunes. The float, shotted down to a quarter of an inch of the surface, to my eye indicated no bite, but invariably, when the end of the swim had been reached, within a foot or so, my good friend was somehow playing a fish, following it hither and thither under the point of his rod. The 20-foot bamboo was unshipped after the orthodox Lea style, reducing its length, and the angler netted his fish without a splash or alarming movement.

The essence of roach fishing, under these circumstances, is to be quiet, and so well did this successful angler comply with the requirement, that a pretty brown water-rat opposite went on diving for, and returning to land with, some kind of ribbon weed, and audibly munching it on the balcony of his sandy abode in the bank. In less than three-quarters of an hour I witnessed, by this clever tight-line fishing, the taking of ten roach, of which the largest was nearly a pound and a half, and the smallest three-quarters of a pound. I enjoyed the watching, I am sure, as much as the veteran enjoyed the catching. As an illustration of the precarious nature of roach fishing, it is incumbent upon me to add that the whole of the morning and afternoon, to that evening hour when the mellow sun was setting over the church spire and its adjacent rookery, had yielded only half-a-dozen small fish.

CHAPTER V.

WINTER.

WHEN the salmon, by legislative enactment, are hunted no more by net or by rod, but are allowed to perform their spawning operations in peace and security; when the trout are also left undisturbed, to increase and multiply, and get into condition by the time that spring returns again, there is still a good deal worth having left for the English angler. Fair-weather fishermen will put away their rods and console themselves during the short winter days, and long winter nights, by their firesides; but there will be in town and country a decided majority of enthusiastic English anglers, who will brave the frost, snow, rain, and fog, and never abandon, until compelled to do so, their raids upon the fish that are in season.

As in treating of the Salmonidæ I have placed the *Salmo salar* at the head of the list, so in a concluding chapter upon winter angling, I cannot do less than give prominence to the pike.

The humanitarian question of angling, I may confess, without apology, never troubles me, and there will be time enough to meet it and deal with it, or shirk it, when, should the Pigeon Shooting Bill become law, consequential attempts are made to interfere in other directions. During the debate in Parliament upon that remarkable measure, it may be remembered that references were made to the pastime of angling. Until actually forced to defend themselves, I should recommend anglers to hold their tongues upon the subject. It is very plausible to argue, as many do, that it is vouchsafed to fishes to enjoy a minimum of pain; and there are some who are so convinced of this great gift to the finny race, that they have at last apparently persuaded themselves that fish rather like the sensation of being hooked and played than otherwise. It may be so. With regard to the pike I do not, however, hesitate to declare that I have no bowels of mercy for him. Last year I read a singularly interesting book by a lady, who described her travels by fell and fiord in Iceland. The authoress was a confessed fly-fisherwoman, and she, as might be expected from one of the tender-hearted sex, seemed to be a little troubled in mind upon the question of cruelty. One argument of hers struck me as being so apposite, that I entered it in my note-book, and, in beginning this chapter, which is virtually one upon pike fishing, I will take the liberty to quote it:—

"Fish are outside our circle altogether, and we may have the further satisfaction of thinking that though they seem to live particularly careless, jolly lives, they all end in being eaten, either by us or by each other, unless they meet with great ill-luck, such as chemical waste in rivers, and are poisoned. Now, for every big fish we kill, and it is these we aim at, a number of merry little fishes have longer lives; so we anglers are really benevolent institutions from a purely fishy point of view. Real fish, too, as distinguished from whales and seals, have no attachment to each other—they are only rivals. Witness the fighting for bait in a shoal; witness the withered old carp wrestling with each other in ancient palace waters. Therefore, in catching a fish you make no home desolate, you bereave no fond creature of a friend. Cool, calm, and selfish, the fish goes on his glittering way like a regular man of the world; he misses nobody out of his water home, and, when he ends an easy life by an easy death, nobody misses him."

The character of the fresh-water shark is especially exemplified in the closing sentence of the extract, and the authoress might have gone further and described *Esox lucius* as a systematic and professional marauder. He respects not his own kith and kin; he prowls up and down, seeking what he may devour; and he has no claim upon our consideration except as a furnisher of sport. There are few waters that are exclusively devoted to the breeding and preservation of pike, and, in the majority of rivers and lakes with which I am acquainted, where they are to be found, keeping down these creatures is a general good.

Spinning is in pike-fishing what the use of the artificial fly is with salmon, trout, and grayling; it is the most artistic branch of the sport. Pike fishers in one respect resemble their brethren of the salmon rod, for they are continually inventing new fancies, laying down new theories, trying new experiments, and dogmatising upon them all with a profundity of faith that in these sceptical days is most refreshing to witness. Artificial baits have been invented without end, and for each and all there is something to be said. I shall not venture to discuss them, but I may remark in passing, that artificial baits, from the oldest to the newest, are very useful to the pike angler.

There are times when it is impossible to procure the natural food of the fish, and there are times, as every angler knows, when a spoon-bait or artificial dace or gudgeon, or one of those beautifully finished imitations of fish in brass, silver, and other less solid compositions, answer better than anything else. But, when the natural baits are to be obtained, let the angler give them a fair trial before he takes out his artificial bait-case. I will illustrate, to the best of my ability, the principal methods of pike-angling by casual recollections which it is pleasant for me to recall.

The first scene is a lake in one of those old English estates which have been in the possession of one family for generations. As I wait for the keeper to open the doors of the boat-house and bring out the little fishing-boat from which I am to operate, I can descry over the tree-tops the turrets of a castle of modern build, and behind me, peeping through the leafless branches of another plantation, I can see, beyond a group of noble cedars, the ivy-covered ruins of a building in which Sir Walter Raleigh spent a portion of his time, and which was made short work of by Cromwell, who placed his cannon upon the hill yonder, at the bottom of which is the deer fence. In the home park a choice herd of Jersey cattle are grazing, and as I put my pike fishing-tackle together, I notice the Squire, an octogenarian within a month or two, drive down the chestnut avenue with his workmanlike four-in-hand.

An angler here, who had the necessary permission, might fish all the year round. Beginning with January, there is not only this lake, with its coarse fish, but a grayling stream within three miles. When, in spring, the trout are in condition, there is a river within an hour's drive behind a fast-stepping dog-cart horse. Roach last until the "ides of March" are over, and they may be caught even in winter in shoals around the promontory on the lawn where the swans are fed. Tench of enormous size infest the waters, biting well in spring, and timing their domestic duties, as an old writer intended them to do, with the blossoming of wheat. The head of the extensive house of Cyprinidæ Brothers may be left out of consideration, for the fat, lazy rascal seldom comes from his hiding-place until the winter is over and gone; yet in the under-keeper's garden there is a rudely-stuffed specimen of a carp of 24 lbs., set up as a scare-crow. Perch may be taken up to the middle of March. By the time trout-fishing is over, which in the stream in question is virtually at the end of July, the coarse fish are ready again, and the grayling almost fit, in the stream into which they were introduced some years ago. There is finally an estuary not very far away where salmon peel are occasionally taken.

The centre, however, of all this fishing is the serpentine lake, out of which, last Christmas, the nephew of the old squire, in a short December afternoon, killed 80 lbs. weight of pike. It is with no ordinary hope, therefore, that I enter the boat and am pushed out upon the surface. Some men are born to be unlucky, and, in angling, I have often thought that I am one of them. There is not to-day a breath of wind to ruffle the surface, or scatter the light mist which still broods over the water. Although the thin blue smoke which floats over the trees from the castle chimneys shows that what little upper current of air there is comes from the bleak north-easterly quarter, which anglers never pray for, there may yet be a chance, for, if the wind be verily honest and constant, you need not, in pike-fishing, seriously trouble as to the point of the compass from which it blows. Wind of some sort, however, is a prime necessity in pike-fishing.

I had rigged up without loss of time my spinning apparatus. As the reader is probably aware, there are many spinning flights of different sizes, of different patterns, but they are all based upon the one supposition that by their means the bait is made to spin without an ugly motion, and as nearly as possible to resemble the swimming of a natural fish. I have tried all the flights that have been invented, and having listened carefully to all the arguments advanced in their favour, have at last decided in favour, first, of one which has no other name, to my knowledge, than "Storr's flight"; and the other, I believe, is called Wood's Chapman spinner. The latter has a lead weight moulded around a length of brass wire, which is sharpened at the end, and armed with a small hook. At the head of the weight are a couple of flanges to give the requisite spinning motion. The sharply-pointed leaded wire, with its little hook, is thrust into the interior of the fish until the flanges protrude on either side of the mouth. Two sets of flights then lie along the sides of the bait. The whole arrangement is of course kept from slipping out by the aforementioned small hook attached to the wire.

This bait spins beautifully, and it has the very desirable advantage of making but one splash when thrown into the water, because, the weight being within the bait, the usual lead attached to the trace, a foot or so from the bait, is dispensed with. The disadvantage of the Chapman spinner is that after being in action a short time the tender interior of the fish with which you are spinning yields to the constant pressure of the tiny hook, and there is a gradual withdrawal of the flanges from the mouth. Still it is an excellent bait, because you can at least make sure that it will always revolve steady and straight, while the disposition of the flights gives the pike very little chance when once he has closed his jaws upon it.

Storr's flight is a simple and convenient, yet at the same time effective, arrangement. It consists of one large triangle, two of the hooks standing out laterally. This is attached to a piece of gimp half an inch longer than the bait to be used. By means of a baiting-needle the gimp is passed through and out of the mouth, the large triangle jamming against the vent, and there remaining. It will be found convenient to have a small triangle attached to an inch and a quarter of gimp, slipping over, and flying loose above the shoulders of the bait. Sometimes a difficulty is found when the bait is other than dace or gudgeon, in getting the proper spinning motion; but you soon learn how to act.

It is always best in pike-fishing to use a trace of twisted gut. Our forefathers considered that anything would do for pike, but this is an exploded idea. The use of coarse gimp is now generally acknowledged to be a mistake, and the deterioration of the quality of gimp some little time ago led to a more general adoption of the twisted or double gut trace. Gimp, however, for the hooks, is essential in angling for a fish with such a formidable furnishing of teeth as the pike.

On a day like the one in which we are supposed to be fishing the Squire's lake, fine tackle is more than ever a necessity, for not only is there an absence of wind, but the water is unfortunately abnormally clear. The direful *anacharis* has, as usual, installed itself in the lake, and, but for the free use of an ingenious steam ploughing machine, would render pike fishing an impossibility, so densely has it taken possession. The first few casts produce nothing. In fact, to be truthful, I must confess that two hours pass before any sign of sport is forthcoming. This in a choice preserve known to be, as the saying goes, full of pike, is ominous, for the voracious nature of the fish is such that if he means taking he does not waste time in pondering over the how and wherefore. But fate relents towards the afternoon, and a pretty ripple dances over the more exposed portions of the lake. A long cast into one of the open spaces brings me the first fish. It moves, nevertheless, in a most mysterious way. Upon feeling the attack you of course strike sharply. Anglers are earnestly impressed with the duty in fishing for pike of striking hard, so as to plunge the barbs into the bony palate; and they are recommended, if in doubt, to strike a second time. There is little necessity for the advice. The rousing shake which a hungry pike gives to a spinning bait acts upon the angler as if he had received a violent blow in the face, and he will assuredly strike back again; in other words, he involuntarily gives his line a quick twitch. The pike then shakes his head angrily, as if he would worry the bait into pieces, and the arm of the angler again involuntarily responds to this by another sharp strike.

Our fish at present, however, seems to be indulging in a relay of rotatory movements that are incomprehensible, but they are partly explained when the captive is brought to the side of the boat; the line is wound six times round the body of the fish so tightly that in one of the circles it has cut into the belly. The boat is next slowly pulled about in the deeper water, where in winter time the fish lie; but the wind has dropped again, and the day seems to yield nothing heavier than seven or eight pounds, and there are only some eight or ten fish lying at the bottom of the half boat half punt. Allusion has been made to a little promontory jutting out from the lawn, at the end of which the food is thrown in for the swans; and although the water there is shallow, it is a reasonable supposition that the clustering of small fry, picking up grains of barley and what not, may have induced a cunning pike to sneak around in the rear. Just half-an-hour before dark, putting this theory to the proof, we get towards that quarter, and a fresh dace, bright as silver, falls into the water about a yard from the land. Apparently from the outer fringe of a mass of decayed weeds, and in not more than a foot depth of water, something arrow-like speeds straight away, churning up the water as it goes. There is no half-heartedness about the smack bang of the transaction.

The fish, as you may wager without seeing the result, has taken every one of the hooks into his safe keeping, and has only to be allowed to take his own course to be added to the spoil already accumulated. Given strong tackle, well tried before the day's angling begins, there is little excuse for the loss, by breaking away, of a well-hooked pike, however large it may be; barring such accidents as fouling with trees, or hanging the line up in some irretrievable position. And a sixteen-pound pike on a spinning flight does not give in all of a moment. Your pike never fights out the battle like some of the fish that have been spoken of in the course of these pages, but he puts out all his strength and speed when hooked only with snap tackle, and is by no means a contemptible antagonist. This fellow leaps out of the water after a thirty yards gallop, and plunges into a weed bank. But I winch up to him in the boat, dislodge him, and gaff him, to put the crowning weight to the sum total, which the keeper's man bears, staggering, away with me in a rush basket to the station.

The venerable practice of trolling with the dead gorge has latterly gone a good deal out of fashion, and it cannot be denied that its deadly nature is a fair argument against it when the preservation of the pike is in question. Let the fish be ever so small, after it has taken the murderous gorge into its gullet, its career is ended, and even pike must have sportsman's law, and the youngsters be returned to the water when possible. But I must plead guilty to a sneaking kindness for this form of pike-fishing, upon which, in the seventeenth century, old Robert Nobbes wrote a very quaint treatise. Trolling is the kind of artifice that suits a half-indolent man, or one who, through age or inclination, does not care to enter into the fatiguing labour which is involved in a day's spinning.

Trolling is an appropriately effective method of angling for pike in a river. The angler, with bag and gaff slung at his back, sallies forth on a winter day, crackling the frozen snow, perhaps, beneath his feet as he trudges to the river-side. His trolling bait may be dropped here and there into holes and eddies, the proceeding being just sufficient to keep his blood in active circulation, the exercise enough to bring all his muscles into play, and yet all being conducted with a dignified action that adds not a little to the enjoyment of the sport. There is also something particularly entertaining in the manner in which the movements of the pike are to be studied when trolling.

You have thrown your bait out ten, twelve, or fifteen yards, as the case may be; it sinks to the bottom, and by a series of gentle draws up and down and ever onwards, it is gradually worked towards you, the line meanwhile being neatly coiled on the ground at your left side, unless you have acquired the art of casting, Nottingham style, from the winch, which is the poetry of the process.

Something on the way seems to touch the bait. Is it a loose weed? It may be a submerged branch. Here, then, is the first sensation—to determine whether the slight check proceeds from a fish. At any rate, you have paused in action. Sometimes the angler is held in doubt for several seconds. The pike on grabbing the bait (across the middle) has a habit of keeping still, as if to gloat over the certainty of a meal which Providence has at last placed in his way. Before long, however, he will begin to move away, the line running meanwhile free through the rings. The art of trolling lies not a little in calculating the amount of freedom which it is necessary to allow the fish. The general rule is that the pike, having struck the bait, proceeds forthwith with the pleasing movement technically known as "a run." The theory is that, not to be disturbed or pounced upon by a big brother, he retires to his lodgings, which may be near or which may be a long distance off, to pouch at leisure.

On no account should the line be checked; and it is the safest plan to allow the fish to pouch at even inordinate leisure, if such be his inclination, and then move off on a second excursion. By this time it will be safe to tighten the line, striking being unnecessary with this particular process, and to bring the fish in. The two hooks are not in trolling affixed to the bony walls of the jaws, but in the soft linings of the gullet, and there is no shaking them off or breaking them. This is the general rule, but the experienced troller is aware that when the pike is a large one it often takes the bait, slews it round, and swallows it at a gulp, and then darts swiftly, and may be repentant, away. Some five or ten minutes are generally consumed in waiting for the moment when it is safe to bring to his senses a fish that has taken your trolling bait in the regular way, and this prolonged sensation of hope and doubt may be fairly set off against the more acute excitement of playing a fish struck with the spinning flights.

The live bait gorge is open to the same objections as are urged against the trolling hook, but it is a very convenient method of commanding broad water upon which there is no boat, and where your float should be despatched on a mission of not less than thirty yards, the line being kept up, while the bait is working, by three or four smaller floats unattached. This is the only justification for using it, there being no ground for the excuse pleaded by the troller, that he can work between weeds and cover water, impracticable for spinning. Jardine's snap-tackle has been now generally adopted, in preference to the saddle and other rigs familiar to pike fishermen for many years.

A final word as to useful winter occupation for the angler. When the low-lying lands are a yellow sea, and the heads of the trees in which you were wont to entangle your fly-cast in the summer, seem to be floating on a watery expanse; when the river has forgotten its bounds, and the landmarks are swept away, there is no angling, save in a few exceptional lakes which never become discoloured. At home, you will be tired, sooner or later, of gazing at those stuffed fish that day by day remind your admiring household of your genius. The fondling of your rods and books, and general impedimenta, palls after a while. But, from the thoroughly practical books which have been published, exhausting every phase of the subject of angling, there is always something to be learned: and in the lighter literature of the sport, which is part study of human nature, part communion with nature, animate and inanimate, other than human, and part rehearsal of angling experiences, we may, through the darkest night and most inclement day, be led to continue our recreation in the spirit, if not in the flesh.

(And Sold at their Stalls near each Entrance to the Exhibition.)

OFFICIAL GUIDE BOOKS, &c.

LARGE PLAN and TOUR of the BUILDINGS, 1d.; post-free 1½d.

GUIDE to the EXHIBITION, 3d.; post-free 4d.

PROGRAMME of MUSIC, &c., 2d.; post-free 3d.

OFFICIAL CATALOGUE, Second Edition, 1s.; post-free 1s. 4d.

CHEAP RECIPES for FISH COOKERY. Prepared by Mrs. CHARLES CLARKE. 3d.; post-free 4d.

THE FISHERIES PORTFOLIO:

CONTAINING

Ten Original Etchings of Scenes on the British Coast.

TITLE.	ARTIST.
1.—Bait Gatherers	R. W. MACBETH, A.R.A.
2.—Running Ashore	COLIN HUNTER.
3.—A Fisher Girl	J. D. WATSON.
4.—Fishing Boats off Hastings	DAVID LAW.
5.—Going for Bait	OTTO LEYDE, R.S.A.
6.—Boat Building on the Yare	C. J. WATTS.
7.—Preparing for Sea—Hastings	C. P. SLOCOMBE.
8.—Ramsgate Harbour	J. P. HESELTINE.
9.—Fisherman's Haven	J. MACWHIRTER, A.R.A.
10.—Stranded—Rye.	WILFRID W. BALL.

Price 15s. the complete set.

LONDON: WILLIAM CLOWES & SONS, LIMITED

PAPERS OF THE CONFERENCE

Held in connection with the GREAT INTERNATI[ONAL]
FISHERIES EXHIBITION.

N[OW READY.]

Demy 8vo., in Illustrate[d Wrapper.]

INAUGURAL MEETING: [Address by]
H.R.H. the PRINCE OF WALES (Presid[ent).]

NOTES ON THE SEA FISHE[RIES AND FISHING FOLK]
OF THE UNITED KINGDOM. By H.R.H THE DUKE OF EDINBURGH, K.G. 1s.

THE FISHERY INDUSTRIES OF THE UNITED STATES. [By Pro-]
fessor BROWN GOODE, M.A.

OYSTER CULTURE AND OYSTER FISHERIES IN THE NE[THER-]
LANDS. By Professor HUBRECHT.

PRINCIPLES OF FISHERY LEGISLATION. By Right Hon. [SHAW]
LEFEVRE, M.P.

ON THE CULTURE OF SALMONIDAE AND THE AC[CLIMA-]
TISATION OF FISH. By Sir JAMES RAMSAY GIBSON MAITLAND, Bart.

FISH DISEASES. By Professor HUXLEY, P.R.S.

THE ECONOMIC CONDITION OF FISHERMEN. By Profess[or]
LEVI.

THE FISHERIES OF CANADA. By L. Z. JONCAS.

PRESERVATION OF FISH LIFE IN RIVERS BY THE E[XCLU-]
SION OF TOWN SEWAGE. By the Hon. W. F. B. MASSEY MAINWARING.

MOLLUSCS, MUSSELS, WHELKS, &c., USED FOR FOOD O[R BAIT.]
By CHARLES HARDING.

COARSE FISH CULTURE. By R. B. MARSTON.

ON THE FOOD OF FISHES. By Dr. F. DAY.

THE HERRING FISHERIES OF SCOTLAND. By R. W. DUFF

LINE FISHING. By C. M. MUNDAHL.

FISH TRANSPORT AND FISH MARKETS. By His Excellency [SPENCER]
WALPOLE.

FOREST PROTECTION AND TREE CULTURE ON [RIVER]
FRONTAGES. By D. HOWITZ, Esq.

SEAL FISHERIES. By Captain TEMPLE.

FISH AS FOOD. By Sir HENRY THOMPSON.

STORM WARNINGS. By R. H. SCOTT.

ON THE DESTRUCTION OF FISH AND OTHER AQ[UATIC]
ANIMALS BY INTERNAL PARASITES. By Professor COBBOLD, F.R.S., F.L.S.

SCIENTIFIC RESULTS OF THE EXHIBITION. By Professor
LANKESTER.

A NATIONAL FISHERY SOCIETY FOR GREAT BRITA[IN. By]
C. E. FRYER.

CRUSTACEANS. By T. CORNISH.

TRAWLING. By ALFRED ANSELL.

THE BASIS FOR LEGISLATION ON FISHERY QUESTIO[NS. By]
Lieut.-Col. F. G. SOLÁ.

MACKEREL AND PILCHARD FISHERIES. By T. CORNISH.

ARTIFICIAL CULTURE OF LOBSTERS. By W. SAVILLE KENT

FRESHWATER FISHING (other than Salmon). By J. P. WHEELDO[N.]

SALMON AND SALMON FISHERIES. By DAVID MILNE HOME,

THE FISHERIES OF IRELAND. By J. C. BLOOMFIELD.

ON IMPROVED FACILITIES FOR THE CAPTURE, ECO[NOMIC]
TRANSMISSION AND DISTRIBUTION OF SEA FISHES, AND HOW [THESE]
MATTERS AFFECT IRISH FISHERIES. By R. F. WALSH, of Kinsale.

IN THE PRESS.

THE FISHERIES OF OTHER COUNTRIES. By Commissi[oners from]
Sweden, Norway, Spain, &c., who took part in the Conference.

LONDON: WILLIAM CLOWES & SONS, LIMITED,